A Piece of Her Heart

The True Story of a Mother and Daughter
Separated by the Russian Revolution and the
Lives Their Families Built While Apart

by Sissy Carpey

iUniverse, Inc.
New York Bloomington

iUniverse books may be ordered through booksellers or by contacting:

iUniverse
1663 Liberty Drive
Bloomington, IN 47403
www.iuniverse.com
1-800-Authors (1-800-288-4677)

Because of the dynamic nature of the Internet, any Web addresses or links contained in this book may have changed since publication and may no longer be valid. The views expressed in this work are solely those of the author and do not necessarily reflect the views of the publisher, and the publisher hereby disclaims any responsibility for them.

ISBN: 978-1-4401-7722-4 (sc)
ISBN: 978-1-4401-7723-1 (ebook)
ISBN: 978-1-4401-7724-8 (hc)

Jews   Eastern Europe   America   Family Memoir

Printed in the United States of America

iUniverse rev. date: 10/12/2009

CONTENTS

Acknowledgements... xi

One — Waiting for a Lost Daughter........................... 1

Two — A Child at My Grandmother's Feet 10

Terror and Death in the *Shtetl* and an American Life 10
One Sad Photograph in a Houseful of Happy Memories 14
How They Lived—From Catherine the Great to the
  Cantonist Years to the *Vereins* in America 16

Three — Tea and Cake and History, Tales from
  the Shtetl 21

Malka and Goddel — A Love Match 28
The Sisters' Stories When it Rained on the Bride and
  Groom 36
Inda Goes to America 39
Yetta—Marriage and Divorce 40
Goddel in the Czar's Army, and a Public Kiss 47
Yetta Goes to America 49

Four — The Good Years Turn to Sorrow and
  Danger 51

A Family Trapped 51
Ida, her Father's Daughter and Mother—Daughter
  Conflicts 52
Pogroms, War and Revolution—the Terrible Days 54
The Cossacks, the Bolsheviks and the Petliura, and the
  Death of a Beloved Father 55
Vodka Saves Them 60

Five — A Mother's Only Choice 65

Six — Two Journeys to Safety 68

Escape to America 68
The Doors Almost Close 71
Survival in Asia 77
A Sacrifice for the Whole Family 79
Tashkent—City of Bread 81

Seven — In America The First Days 84

Eight — American Courtships, American Lives 94

Young Love in America 97
The Old Customs Die Slowly 102
Hard Times in America 105
Finding My Sister 106
The Great Depression and the American Generation 109
Malka's Sons and Their American Born Wives 112

Nine — The Family Threads Are Cut 121

Ten — Our American Childhoods 126

Living Behind the Store 126
The Smells and Sounds of a Jewish Neighborhood 129
Remember the Sabbath and Keep it Holy 131
Malka—Citizenship Class and Suitors 131
On the Boardwalk in Atlantic City and My Grandmother's
  Boarding House 134

**Eleven — Our Sick Brother and World War Two
  Memories 137**

Summers at the Seashore—and the End of the War 140

**Twelve — The Russian Family—Did the Nazis
  Kill Them? 145**

Thirteen — Moon over Miami 147

Leaving Her Sick Child 147
Another Separation of the Family 149

Fourteen — Enemies, Once a Family 154

Fifteen — Life in the Tropics 157

Our Sick Brother is Well 157
The Poor Relatives 161

Sixteen — All the Young Men are in Uniform Again... 165

Love and Marriage...167
Interference and Advice..173
The *Knipple*... 175

Seventeen — Family Togetherness 177

Eighteen — Our Lost and Found Aunt 180

Part of the Family at Last..186
Another Sad Farewell and a New Beginning.....................189

Nineteen — A Daughter Found, A Daughter Lost. 191

Twenty — Family Circle—1975.............................. 196

Twenty One — Full Circle 199

Israel—1977 199
New York—2007...204

Epilogue — 2009.. 206

Appendix 208

Frima and Yisroel's Escape from Russia..........................209

To My Grandchildren

Rachel Fayth
Andrew Brett
Valerie Joy
Caroline Sarah
Benjamin Kane
Julia Blair
Emily Rose

Know those who came before you

ACKNOWLEDGEMENTS

PERHAPS FIVE YEARS AGO, when I audited several Jewish Studies courses at the University of Pennsylvania, I told one of my professors, Dr. Benjamin Nathans, that I had interviewed and taped my grandmother and aunts and knew about the lives they had lived in the shtetl before and during the Soviet Revolution. He responded, "You are sitting on very important material."

I realized at that moment that I must write this book. I am grateful to Dr. Nathans for that encouraging statement.

My daughter, Jodi Greenspan, and her daughter, Rachel, were my two strong right hands during these years of research and writing. I could not have completed this project without their honest critiques and their belief in me. Jodi was my editor, and Rachel was her partner. They also walked me through many computer problems. They were my first readers, and great sounding boards.

All of my grandchildren were involved in this project. Valerie Carpey put together the family tree. Caroline Carpey prepared my Power Point presentation of photos from the Ukrainian towns of our family. Andrew Greenspan, Benjamin Carpey, Julia and Emily Carpey listened, asked questions, and helped me bridge the gap between their generation and the generations before them.

My husband, Al, though he tried to lure me away from my work at a reasonable hour, encouraged me always, and I thank you, Al, for your loving support, even when I went to the Ukraine and Russia without you.

Thanks to my cousin, Diane Kamis Wasserman, who found priceless family photos hidden in drawers and corners, including a photograph taken when our parents were toddlers in the *shtetl*, and to my cousin, Judith Nissman Miller, for giving me the wedding portrait of her grandparents, Yetta and Moishe Adelman, with Moishe's three motherless children.

Thanks to my cousin, Israel Bogdonoff, who, when in his 90's, handed me the memoir he wrote about his childhood in the shtetl and escape to America with his mother.

Every woman in my writers' group was a resource to me, giving me practical advice and editorial honesty. Still, there were a few special moments. Once, my fellow writer, Nimisha Ladva, holding her sleeping baby in her arms as I read the first chapters of the book to the group, stood still for 20 minutes as I read, and said, "Keep writing, Sissy." Then she hurried home with her baby. Thanks to Joyce Eisenberg, who invited me to join the writers' group, and was always willing to share her editing skills with me. Thanks, too, to Elizabeth Cantonese, a graduate student at Bryn Mawr College, my first editor.

ONE — WAITING FOR A LOST DAUGHTER

DURING THE KOREAN WAR, IN 1951, my brother, Norman, was investigated for top secret clearance. He had enlisted in the Air Force, and was assigned to the Atomic Energy Commission. It was at the height of the Cold War and the hysteria of the McCarthy era.

Federal investigators knocked on our neighbors' doors and visited our high school. They asked questions about my brother's patriotism. Had he ever expressed any sympathy for Communism?

Other FBI investigators grilled my brother. One day, they said to him, "We know that your mother has a sister in the Soviet Union. What would you do if a Soviet agent came to you and told you that your aunt and her family would be killed unless you gave the Russians some information?"

"I would say 'Kill them all,'" my brother responded. "I am an American." When he came home on leave, he told us the story. Our mother, Florence, nodded her head in passionate agreement.

"You did the right thing," she said. "This sister in Russia, what is she to me? Would I know her? Would she know me? Do I even know if she is alive?"

She knew her once as her oldest sister, Frayda. Her big sister had braided her baby hair, tickled her until she laughed, and hidden with her during the Bolshevik Revolution. But that was in another life.

My brother and I and all our cousins grew up knowing there was a branch of our family in Russia. Our parents never talked about them. There were no letters. We didn't know where they lived, or how they lived, or if they lived.

There was, however, one photograph. It had a place among the pictures of smiling brides and grooms and curly-haired toddlers covering every inch of space on my grandmother's dining room buffet, spilling over to flat surfaces like window sills and coffee tables, each photograph another piece of our family's life. Except this one.

There was something mysterious about this picture. Mysterious and sad. The photo was done in that somber brownish black and white, sepia, which is once again in vogue in art photography. The sadness did not come from the photographic process. It was the people who were sad. Four people— Frayda, her husband, little girl and little boy, looked straight at us with no expression in their faces, no life in their eyes. Those faces hid more than they told, but what they told was that theirs was a life so different from ours that despite a certain look to the eyes, a certain shape to the face, these were not our people. Only there, in my grandmother's dining room display, were they part of our family.

At the height of the Cold War, my mother agreed with her son. There was no need for my brother or our government to concern themselves with the possible Russian agent. The sister in Russia was probably dead. How could she have survived the Nazis? And if she lived, what was she to us?

Then, in 1963, a dozen years after my brother's experience, almost a half century after Malka, my grandmother, had shepherded four of her children to America, a letter came from our lost aunt, Malka's lost daughter.

My aunt and her family were alive. They had left the *shtetl* (village where Jews lived) in the Russian Pale of Settlement and settled in Tashkent, in Uzbekistan. If they had remained in the *shtetl*, the Nazis would have killed them, as they killed all the Jews in the villages and towns of the Ukraine. The Nazis never got to Tashkent.

My aunt was a midwife, her husband a tailor. The little girl and little boy in the photograph in my grandmother's dining room were both doctors, one a pediatrician, the other a gynecologist.

Malka's chest swelled with pride as she listened to my father read the letter, written in Yiddish. There were no doctors yet in our family. Who could believe that from her oldest child, the one trapped in the *shtetl*, would come such news?

In the letter, there was one refrain that was repeated. If her mother still lived, my aunt wrote, in the moving Yiddishisms of her childhood, she would like to see her once more before she died.

The Korean War was long over. The Cold War showed signs of a thaw. While the United States and the Soviet Union did not trust each other, and the people living under Soviet rule lived in a police state, it had been years since the Soviet Prime Minister, Nikita Khrushchev, warned American President Richard Nixon, "We will bury you!" The Iron Curtain was still closed shut, but there were places worn thin enough to see through.

Now, our aunt in Russia was real to us. And to our mother, she was a sister again, not a vague memory. My youngest uncle went to Washington to arrange for the visit of his sister to America. He saw his congressman. He went to the State Department. Our aunt, on the other side of the world, wrote that she needed an official invitation from us.

It took a long time, almost two years, to cut through the red tape on both sides. The letters kept coming, each one with photos of the family we had never expected to know. A 12-year-old girl, her hair in two long, dark pigtails, just as mine had been when I was her age. Boys who had none of the mischief in their eyes that their American cousins had, boys who didn't seem to know how to smile, their parents posing just as solemnly. In none of the letters did they write about Siberia, of hunger, of fear. That we would learn later.

The sad, solemn family in Tashkent.
The first family photo they sent.

We responded with our own letters and photographs. In every letter the American family sent, all written in Yiddish, the only language we shared, we asked what our lost family needed. Could we send a package to them in the Soviet Union? Our aunt ignored those questions.

Malka, a woman almost 80, took matters into her own hands early in the correspondence. Uneducated as she was, unable to read in any language, she did her research by talking to people— the rabbi at the synagogue, the immigrant women who were her friends, the ladies who sat next to her in the beauty shop each week.

One morning, dressed for a day in downtown Philadelphia, her gray-white hair set an hour earlier at the beauty shop, her nails perfectly manicured, her lips bright with color, (Malka always thought of herself as the beautiful young woman she had once been, and took pride in her appearance) my grandmother boarded two trolley cars to the shopping center of the city and walked into a small travel agency that had a connection to the Soviet Union. It was owned by a Jewish man who, from the moment of the first tear in the Iron Curtain, did business with the Communists. Though he was a travel agent, he knew what the Russian people needed, and how to get it to them.

Malka called her sons and told them she needed money to send warm, wool blankets to their sister. From that moment on, Malka visited her new friend every month, with money from her sons in her handbag. She knew, and so did the rest of us, that some of those blankets would be used for barter, that they might make our lost family's life a bit easier.

We waited for the letter that would tell us when our aunt was coming to America.

Now, on a hot May evening in 1965, an evening more like summer than spring, my mother, Florence, her sister, Ida, and her brothers, Lou and Charles, were at Kennedy

Airport in New York. Ida's daughter, Pearl, and her husband, Morrie, had driven them there in their big, white Cadillac.

Back in Philadelphia, Malka sat in the middle of her narrow street on a lawn chair, holding court as if she was the queen of the prom. She was dressed in a crisp and spotless summer dress, one of the many in her wardrobe. The family, aunts and uncles and cousins with their toddlers and babies, was gathering. Among them was my brother, Norman, and his wife and baby. Norman, who had been asked what he would do if a Soviet agent threatened to kill his aunt in the Soviet Union, would soon embrace that aunt.

All the neighbors were on their porches, eager to be part of the drama. Friends from around the corner and down the street stopped at my grandmother's lawn chair, as if they just happened to stroll by on an evening walk. As if she always parked a chair in the middle of the street.

A reporter and photographer from a Philadelphia newspaper showed up and introduced themselves to Malka. She quickly ordered me to bring chairs to the street for her guests. Though she had not expected them, and had never been interviewed before, she answered their questions like an experienced hand at press relations. I listened as she told them what I had always known. She had fled for her life with four of her five children during the Soviet Revolution because the Bolsheviks were after them, and during the long years of Stalin and Hitler, when she never heard from her daughter, she thought her child was not alive.

In the middle of the interview, she turned to me again.

"Bring some cold drinks to my guests," she told me, "And some fruit."

I went to the kitchen and filled up two trays, one for the reporters, and one for the rest of us. Especially for our little ones, who were getting restless.

We were all restless. And nervous. The jokes started flying across my grandmother's narrow cement mini-patio that was serving as a grandstand. The cousins, waiting impatiently on that patio, bantered about the Cadillac, the ultimate symbol of capitalism, in which our communist aunt would be riding. Just by chance, several of the young men were wearing red cotton knit shirts. They wore red, the color associated with communist Russia, to welcome her, my cousin Phil suggested, and that brought more jokes.

Meanwhile, at Kennedy Airport, the excitement grew. My mother, upon learning that her sister was actually coming to America, insisted, "How do I know it will be her? The last time I saw her, she had long braids down her back. She was 18 years old. They could send anybody." Now, she stood silently watching the passengers file into Customs, their arms heavy with baggage. She watched the weary passengers lift their ragged bags to the Customs counter. And suddenly, she recognized the sister she was certain she would not know. Frayda was still behind the Customs gate when her youngest sister, my mother, Florence, ran toward the barrier separating them, and, in her excitement, fell on the airport's concrete floor. She cut her chin badly enough to be taken to the infirmary.

Soon, for the first time in half a century, the three sisters and two brothers were together. My cousin, Pearl, reported that they did not stop talking for one moment all the way to Philadelphia. The three sisters sat in the back seat of the car holding hands. The two brothers were on their knees, up front, facing their sisters for the whole 90 miles.

On the long, narrow street in Philadelphia, dusk was turning to night. The neighbors on their porches were still waiting. More relatives came. Our toddlers were sleepy and impatient. We had been waiting for hours.

Then, the car turned the corner into my grandmother's street, and my cousin, seated in the back with the three sisters, reached over her husband's shoulder and put her hand on the horn and held it there. Suddenly, the back door of the Cadillac opened. A solid, elderly woman jumped out of the still moving car, and ran toward my grandmother at the other end of the street. At the same moment, Malka leaped out of her chair and ran toward her daughter.

We all heard the cries, "Momma! Momma! Momma!"

They embraced in the middle of the street.

The next few moments are a noisy, disorganized, joyful haze in my memory. I remember saying to my aunt, as I kissed her, "Aunt, I am Sissy, your sister Fayga's daughter." Everybody else reached out to her at the same time. Her mother, her protector for the first time in so many years, held her close and led her through the crowd into the house.

In minutes, my grandmother's small house was filled with people, the curious as well as family. The reporter and photographer were at Frayda's side, as her brother explained in Yiddish that they wanted to interview her. Her face changed, and she bolted up the stairs in a house she had never seen, crying *"Ich bin nicht political!"*

"I am not political!"

She ran into a bedroom and locked the door behind her. The crowd was silenced immediately.

There were those among us who realized, in that moment, how different her world was from ours. She had run up the stairs in fear. This reporter, this photographer, could make of the reunion a piece of anti-Soviet propaganda. She had a family of her own. She would return to them after this visit. And she knew, from terrifying experience, what could happen to her husband, her children, her grandchildren in the Soviet Union if she brought dishonor upon her country. My uncle, in the innocence and openness of his American life, saw a newspaper story. She saw a political statement.

"Ich bin nicht political."

Her brothers and sisters and their mother quietly and calmly spoke to my aunt through the bedroom door, persuading her to let them in. She opened the door. Soon, my younger uncle, Charles, came down the steps and explained to the members of the Philadelphia press that she was afraid to be interviewed. He thanked them for their interest, got a promise from them to drop the story, and escorted them out of the house. He sent all the neighbors and strangers away.

We stayed a few minutes longer, silently waiting in the living room. Then someone suggested that we leave, that we give mother and daughter time alone before we descended upon them. There was plenty of time to get to know our aunt.

Two — A Child at My Grandmother's Feet

Terror and Death in the *Shtetl* and an American Life

MY GRANDMOTHER, MALKA, WHO WAS "Bubbe" to me from the moment I knew who she was until the day she died in her 97th year, was a story teller. Malka was my mother's mother. As a young widow, she ran from the *shtetl* with four of her young children and no papers during the turmoil and anarchy of the Russian Revolution. It took her almost three years to get from the *shtetl* to the ship that would take them to America. In each town along the way, she farmed out her children to separate Jewish homes. The youngest, Somela, later to be known as Charles, stayed with her, sleeping by her side near the stove in the houses where she was a cook, hidden in another corner of another house, always by her side. The other three earned their keep in strangers' homes as housemaids and roofer's assistant. They were careful not to talk to each other, not to embrace their mother at a chance meeting. Separated, each could pass as belonging to the family who had taken them in. Together, they would be noticed as strangers, as a family of outsiders. They could be sent back to the Bolshevik government they had fled, or jailed for crossing borders without permits.

Bubbe's husband, my grandfather Goddel, died long before she took their children and left the *shtetl*. He had gone to synagogue to say *kaddish* (the prayer for a dead relative) one night, and Ukrainian killers who were followers of a vicious Ukrainian revolutionary, Symon Petliura, interrupted the congregants' prayers. They herded the men to the Jewish cemetery, and set them to work digging their own graves. Then, one of the Ukrainian men recognized my grandfather as someone he knew. He told my grandfather to run as fast as he could and go to every Jewish house and collect all the gold and silver, jewels and money and if there was enough when he returned to the cemetery and if his fellow congregants were still alive, they would let the Jews live.

My grandfather ran like a racehorse all through the night, rushing into houses, filling his arms and his pockets with gold and silver coins and jewelry, candlesticks and *kiddush* cups, wedding rings and necklaces. Women took the earrings from their ears and handed them to my grandfather. My grandfather ran back to the cemetery, his arms and pockets heavy with the load that might mean life to his fellow worshippers. The men, covered with the mud and muck of the holes they were digging, were still alive. The captors kept their word. The Jewish men were released.

My grandfather took to his bed and died two days later. He was 34 years old.

Before he died, he called his oldest son, Labe, who was nine years old, to his bedside, and asked him to promise to take care of my grandmother always. It was a promise my uncle kept all his life.

11

Did my grandfather die of a heart attack from the fright, as my mother told me, or did he die of a fever, an epidemic? My mother's sister, Ida, insisted that diphtheria was in every house in the *shtetl*, in every house he ran in and out of. There are no medical records to check. When his two youngest children, my mother and her brother, Somela, died of heart disease before they reached old age, I saw this as medical evidence. There was a family history of cardiac disease that could be traced back to Goddel. But Aunt Ida was certain her father died of the fever.

If my grandmother was the story teller, I was the listener. As a little girl, I sat at her green Formica-topped kitchen table with its shiny chrome legs in her spotless, sunny kitchen, my bubbe as spotless in her "house dress," her hair covered with a chiffon scarf so that not one strand fell into her dough. I sat quietly as her flour-coated hands held the fragile strudel dough in the air, as she stretched it until it was transparent, as she mixed and tasted this and that.

She lived with us until I was 10 or 11, and later, when she married, she lived only a few city blocks away. I took the short walk to Bubbe's house as many days as I could. There were always homemade cookies. There was usually strudel, and soup, and stories.

The stories she told were more often about the good days than the bad.

Even when she was baking or cooking, my grandmother was dressed for company, her gold hoop earrings sparkling at her earlobes, her hair freshly set at the beauty shop on the corner, her high cheekbones accented with a touch of color, always lipstick on her lips. If the doorbell rang and a "lady friend" or a grandchild stopped by, she removed her apron and welcomed her guest.

I was the granddaughter who stopped by the most. I was also the granddaughter who asked questions, or perhaps I was simply a good listener.

In my grandmother's kitchen, as I watched her knead her dough, or chop her vegetables, I learned about the generations who had come before me.

She would, in Yiddish, describe the furniture her father, Itzak *stolyar*, had made for her when she and my grandfather, Goddel, married. *Stolyar*, I learned at a very early age, translates to "carpenter" in Yiddish. And Itzak was a craftsman, an artist, not merely a carpenter, my grandmother insisted.

With her hands white with flour, she pointed to the dining room.

"My child," she insisted, "This is nothing compared to the furniture I had in Sobolifka. My china closet was of such beautiful wood, and it was twice as wide and twice as tall as this one. And you should have seen the carvings. My father was not only a carpenter, he was an artist, and the men who worked for him were also artists."

"Oh, my child," she sighed, as she described each room, each piece of furniture, the home she had shared with Goddel. It was as if she had left them the week before.

Every time she told me these stories, I asked myself, "If everything was so wonderful, why had they come to America?" I was sure she was making it up.

They hadn't all come to America. In 1920, when she ran from the *shtetl*, my grandmother left her oldest child, Frayda, there. It would be almost a half century before mother and daughter touched again.

She never talked about Frayda. I don't remember any of them talking about Aunt Frayda in all the years of Saturday and Sunday afternoons together as a family. Every week, after my grandmother remarried, we gathered at her house. Before that, when she lived with us, the family crowded into our small living quarters behind the kosher butcher store where my father made his living. Sometimes, we got together at the home of another aunt and uncle, behind the grocery store, the candy store, the cleaning and pressing shop.

And when we came together, we ate. Even through the Depression of the 1930's, we all ate well. Our parents, who remembered the hungry days of Europe, never skimped on food. There was fresh butter and sour cream, homemade soups and noodle *kugels* (Jewish cuisine, a hearty, sweet noodle pudding, with apples and raisins, or sour cream and farmer cheese). Seven days a week, our mothers and aunts cooked and baked and went next door to the grocery store or two doors away to the fruit store to buy the freshest eggs and berries and grapes and melons for their American children. Though the younger cousins wore the older cousins' hand-me-down clothes and none of us had birthday parties, we were rich in family as well as food. There were aunts and uncles and great aunts and uncles. Visiting cousins from Baltimore and New York. Weddings and bar mitzvahs to which all the children were invited.

What we had was family togetherness, except for Aunt Frayda, of course.

One Sad Photograph in a Houseful of Happy Memories

In the early 1940's, my grandmother left us to move a few blocks away to the home she shared with her new husband. It was a corner house on a small street just a few steps from Roosevelt Boulevard in the northeast area of Philadelphia. Roosevelt Boulevard was then, and is now, a wide, many-laned highway. Its other name is Route One, still a major road on the map. In those days, if you were driving south from New York through Philadelphia, or north from Baltimore or Washington, you drove almost past my grandparents' house.

My new grandfather, Philip Savransky, was a distinguished, tall man who, like my grandmother, had lived through war and revolution in Russia. His first wife died there, and he took his only child, a daughter, to America. He married again, had a son, and buried his second wife. At the bar mitzvahs and weddings of Philip's grandchildren, my grandmother is seated in the front row of every formal photograph, dressed in an appropriately beautiful dress, her gray-white hair in a beauty shop hairdo. In the photos of our family affairs, our *zayda* (grandfather) Philip sits in a similar place of respect. He was always, until he got too frail, given the honor of holding the newborn grandsons and great grandsons at each baby's circumcision.

When they married, she moved into his house and made it her home. I missed her. I walked to her house often. It was only three short blocks away. It was not the smells and tastes in her square, sunny kitchen that drew me to her, though she was so good at baking and cooking that my Uncle Lou, who in Europe had been Labe, regretted they had not become caterers when they came to America. They would have all been rich, he was sure.

It was the stories she told that drew me to her kitchen.

Between them, my bubbe and Philip had six children in America, all with spouses. My bubbe had eleven grandchildren, and my zayda had five. Later, when the great grandchildren came, they had an ongoing argument as he counted her grandchildren and great grandchildren—there were many more on her side, and she would angrily respond, "*Dertzail nit mine eyniklach.*" (Do not count my grandchildren.) It was considered bad luck to count people, and she was superstitious. If you have to count, you fool

15

the angel of death by putting a negative in front of each number. "Not one, not two, not three," until you get to the full count.

My bubbe's house was filled with photos of all the children and grandchildren she would not count. The photo gallery was a mirror of the life cycle of the family. There were informal photos of curly haired babies and of the same babies, now toddlers or awkward teenagers, at the beach, at family picnics, or all lined up in front of our grandmother's house. Later, the same toddlers posed for formal bar mitzvah and wedding photos, their parents, older, graying, overweight and American, standing beside them.

The lost family, the family in Russia, was frozen in the moment of the only portrait we had. That photo stood by itself on a small window sill at the right corner of the dining room. To us, they were always a little girl, a little boy, and two young parents, all of them staring somberly at us. None of them were included in the count of "not one, not two," of my grandmother's children and grandchildren.

Why didn't my mother and her siblings talk about their lost sister in all the years of my childhood? How could my grandmother have tucked away the memory of the daughter who was her first child? How could she see that photo every day and yet never speak of Frayda? They, especially my grandmother, must have buried her deep within their hearts so that they could cope with the sorrow, the loss, and the guilt of being safe in America.

How They Lived—From Catherine the Great to the Cantonist Years to the *Vereins* in America

My grandmother Malka, daughter of Esther and Itzak, was born in 1883 in the town of Heisin in the region of the

Ukraine known today as it was then, as Podolia Gubernia, the province of Podolia. Podolia was part of the Pale of Settlement, which stretched from the Baltic Sea in the north to the Black Sea in the south, and was the only part of the Russian Empire where Jews were permitted to live. The Pale of Settlement was created in 1791, when Catherine the Great restricted her Jewish subjects to the territories annexed from Poland on the western border to the territories taken from the Turks along the shores of the Black Sea. When my grandmother was a small child, there were more than two and a half million Jews living in the Pale of Settlement. The numbers doubled in the years of her childhood. According to historians, by 1900, there were five million Jews in the Pale of Settlement.

Despite sporadic pogroms, and the first big wave of immigration to the United States from Eastern Europe, the Russian Jewish population continued to grow. So, also, did the population of other ethnic groups in Eastern Europe. This has been attributed to improved health care and hygiene, and lower infant mortality rates. The Jewish population growth may also have been linked to religious laws governing sexual relations between husband and wife. Women went to a ritual bath, the *mikvah*, several days after their menstrual period ended before resuming the sexual relationship. By then, the Jewish wife was ovulating, ripe for fertilization. Birth rates were high, and improved medical care led to a greater infant survival rate.

Heisin, where my grandmother was born, was a small city, not a village. As the Industrial Revolution spread all over the world, even to the Pale of Settlement, Heisin became a manufacturing town, a center of the clothing industry in pre-revolutionary Russia. Heisin was the district capital. According to records at The Museum of the Diaspora in Tel Aviv, Israel, there were 65 Jews in Heisin in 1765. By 1897, the Jewish population was 4,321,

46% of the city's population. Despite the great waves of immigration to America during those years, there were 5,190 Jews in Heisin in 1926.

During World War Two, Heisin was a Nazi labor camp where Nazi uniforms were made. The slave laborers were the local Jews as well as Romanian Jews who were transported there in trains. Few survived the Holocaust.

I didn't learn that my grandmother was born in Heisin until the day I brought a tape recorder and notebook to her apartment. The only town I had ever heard about from her was Sobolifka.

She was by then living in the senior citizen building where she had moved after her husband, Philip, died. I had prepared her for my mission on the telephone. "Bubbe," I said, "I am coming to learn about the family and about Sobolifka." She was in her 90's by then, and had buried her two youngest children, one of whom was my mother. It wasn't until that day, at my bubbe's kitchen table, that I learned that Heisin, the town where Bubbe was born and also where my father and his family had come from, was close to Sobolifka. As much as they had talked about the old country, about Heisin on my father's side and Sobolifka on my mother's, neither family ever told us that the towns were perhaps fifteen miles from each other.

They were all in their graves when I picked up a copy of Sholem Aleichem's short story collection, *Tevya The Dairyman and the Railroad Stories*. Though I had first read Sholem Aleichem's stories as a teenager, among the railroad stories I had missed was one about a train that stopped at both my mother's and my father's towns.

In a new translation of this collection by Hillel Halkin[1], I read the story, "The Miracle of Hoshana Rabbah." I was

1   Sholem Aleichem, *Tevya The Dairyman and the Railroad Stories*, translated by Hillel Halkin (New York: Schocken Books Inc., 1987), 186.

startled to read, in the first paragraph, "The whole thing happened, don't you know, right in Heysin. That is, not in Heysin itself but a few stops away, in a place called Sobolivka." (There is more than one correct spelling of the towns' names.)

That explained how my mother and father began their courtship at a neighborhood dance in the immigrant neighborhood of South Philadelphia a few years after they came to America. My mother told me that they met, and danced, and she didn't know how it happened, but by the end of the evening she was sitting on his lap. It wasn't a neighborhood dance. More likely, the dance was sponsored by "The Heisiner Benevolent Association."

Everyone in both my father's and mother's family belonged to the "Heisiner Benevolent Association," a *verein* or mutual aid society founded by my father's father, Nathan, whom I never knew.

The Heisiner Benevolent Association later broke into two separate groups. The breakaway group became the Heisiner Independent Young Men's Association. My father was one of the young men.

When I was growing up, my parents took me with them to the meetings and banquets of the Heisiner Independent Young Men's Society. The independent young men from Heisin are all in their graves now, the graves they bought through the *verein* in their younger days. Through the *verein*, they also borrowed money to become small businessmen—butchers and dairymen, grocers and tailors. They took loans from the *verein* to pay for their sons' bar mitzvah parties and their daughters' weddings. The society was one of hundreds of organizations founded by immigrants to help each other take small steps toward success in American life, while they held on to the traditions and culture of the old country. The *vereins* were almost family banks. Members bought shares, just as today's investors buy shares in a public company. A shareholder took a loan and paid it off with interest. The interest gave the *verein* money for investments and social events. Usually, the first official investment was a block of lots in a Jewish cemetery.

Three — Tea and Cake and History, Tales from the Shtetl

The day I walked into my grandmother's apartment with my notebook and tape recorder, she was dressed, as always, for company, in a brightly patterned, crisply-ironed house dress. Her gold hoop earrings still glowed from her ears. But everything hung on her, the dress, the earlobes.

She still went to the beauty shop regularly, and had replaced the house dresses I remembered with new ones which fit her shrinking body. Though the paper thin skin of her hands was wrinkled and her fingers were stiff with age, her nails were manicured and polished a bright red.

When I was newly married, she advised me, "When your husband comes home from work, you must put on a pretty face, with fresh make up. You must always have on a nice dress and a clean apron if you are in the kitchen. Do not be one of those wives who turn into *shtinkers* " (sloppy housewife, unkempt woman).

At 90, though she was no longer preparing for a husband, she continued to start each day dressed for company, always ready for a visit from a grandchild or a neighbor. And if no one called and no one came, the effort was not a waste. She cared about how she looked until the last hours of her long life.

We sat down together at her tiny table in her corner of a kitchen, a kitchen designed for an old woman who wasn't expected to cook or bake, who had no one to care for, no one to cook for. But Malka wasn't an ordinary 90 year old woman.

She busied herself setting the table with the dishes I remembered from the days of my childhood, when I sat at a different kitchen table watching her hands at work and drinking in her stories. The delicate looking, yet sturdy, china was a gift from one of the many young men in our family who fought in World War Two. When the war ended, American soldiers purchased bargains like my grandmother's china from the defeated Japanese and German people. I was in her kitchen the day she opened the carton from Japan. I helped her unwrap the fragile cups and saucers, the serving plates, all with figures of graceful oriental women in flowing orange and blue robes. In another home, those dishes would have stood untouched in a glass-fronted china closet. My grandmother used them every day.

She filled one of the plates with the cookies she always had on hand, and added the fancier pastries she had baked the day before in anticipation of my visit. I watched patiently, waiting for her next step. She reached into another cookie tin for the strudel. There was always a tin of strudel in her freezer. I knew she had removed this one the day before, and that she would insist that I take a few pieces home to my husband.

She bustled around the small kitchen, brought a jar of Nescafe to the table (Malka never brewed coffee), and filled her teapot with water.

In my bubbe's house, you started with food.

But I was there for history, so I set up the tape recorder, opened my notebook and began the interview.

"Tell me about your grandparents," I suggested. "What were their names? Were they born in Sobolifka?"

She did not remember her father's parents' names, nor was she clear on the town they had come from. She was certain it was near Heisin.

She remembered more about her maternal grandparents. Their names, she told me, were Chaika Lea and Usha Krutchikov, and they were Heisiners. Usha was a trader in grains.

"My grandfather went to the peasants and bought the wheat and corn and barley they grew," she explained. "Then he took it to the mill. There, it was made into baking flour. My *zayda* and his workers packaged the flour into sacks and took them to the *yaridim*, the markets, where he sold the sacks to the people. People bought many sacks, to make bread and cakes."

Every town had a market day once a week. Some Jewish merchants, like Usha Krutchikov, traveled from town to town, selling their products on the market days.

The peasants, who lived in the countryside outside the towns, came to the weekly markets to sell the fruits of their labor to the Jews.

And on a good market day, when the peasant or the merchant had a few extra coins jingling in his pocket, the sellers of trinkets, yard goods, and fancy cookies also did well.

Her father, Itzak Feinstein, who was always referred to in family lore as Itzak *stolyar*, Itzak the carpenter, married her mother, Esther Krutchikov, probably around 1878. The first three children in the family, Dvora, Channa, and my grandmother, Malka, were born in Heisin.

The family moved to the *shtetl* of Sobolifka after Malka was born, because her father, she said, had work in Sobolifka.

I think of it as moving from one town to another. But that is because I live in a time of telephones and automobiles, jet planes and email. I rethink it, and realize that though the famous Yiddish writer, Sholem Aleichem, wrote about a train that stopped at the two towns, though the new railroad tracks made it easier to stay in touch with relatives from a nearby town, my great grandparents, Itzak and Esther, left generations of family when they left Heisin, and raised their children without those generations around them.

From the bits and pieces of the old lady's memory, I build a history.

I am still trying to get the genealogy and geography straight when she interrupts me.

"Mein tatta hut alla mol dertzailed unz di myseh fun a bruder, efsher acht yor alt, hut im g'khapped fin cheder tsa di Czar's army."

"My father always talked about his older brother, who was *g'khapped fin cheder* (taken from school) to the Czar's army when he was eight years old, and was never seen or heard from again. His mother died a year later from the heartbreak."

The time line is right. My grandmother was born in 1883. She was the third child in her family. Her parents grew up during the final years of the regime of Nicholas 1, who ruled from 1825 to 1855. Her father's older brother could have been one of the thousands of young Jewish boys who disappeared into the army forever during Nicholas's time. Czar Nicholas 1, one of the most anti-Semitic czars, decreed a twenty-five year draft for Jewish boys as a way of destroying their ties to their people. Some were taken before they reached puberty. There were *khappers*,

Yiddish for "grabbers," members of the Jewish community who filled Nicholas' quota for each town by kidnapping the unlucky young boys. These Jewish boys were sworn into the Czar's Army in the synagogue.

Those who were taken as children were called Cantonists. Most of the Cantonists disappeared into the army and were lost, killed in battle or by the cruelty of the Jew-hating officers and Russian and Ukrainian peasants who were also drafted. Those few who survived became like the men with whom they lived. They abandoned Jewish ways, ate food that was not kosher, and learned to be soldiers, killers. There was no way to celebrate the Jewish Sabbath. Forced conversions to Russian Orthodoxy were common.

Jewish grandmothers have handed down stories of mothers or fathers who cut off a boy child's thumb or forefinger so that he could not hold a rifle, or maimed a son in other ways to keep him out of the Czar's army.

Though the Cantonist laws were repealed in 1856, a year after Nicholas's death, the collective memory of the Jews was that service in the Czar's army was a death sentence for Jewish boys and young men. As late as pre revolutionary times in Russia, many young Jewish boys were maimed by their own families, or sent alone to America when they were young teenagers, to escape the Czar's Army. In my own family, one cousin insists that her father, Uncle Abe, my grandmother's only brother, was sent to America with two young cousins to escape the Czar's army. Immigration records show that Uncle Abe, Abraham Feinstein, of Sobolifka, Russia, entered America on March 6, 1914. He was 20 years old. He came directly to the Port of Philadelphia from Bremen, Germany on the ship, the Brandenburg. The person who sponsored him, and is listed on his immigration record, is Morris Adelman, who was married to Uncle Abe's older sister, Yetta.

After 1856 and through the reign of the last czar, Nicholas III, Jewish boys were drafted for the same term as other Russian draftees, usually five years. But five years in the Czar's army was, for a Jewish young man, still a nightmare, if not always a death sentence.

My grandmother Malka was one of six daughters and one son of Itzak and Esther Feinstein, my maternal great grandparents. Esther, for whom I am named, gave birth to her first three daughters in Heisin, the younger three and only son, Avromele, in Sobolifka, the *shtetl* the family moved to because Itzak found work there.

If my great grandmother gave birth to other children who died in childhood, which is likely, their names and stories have not been passed down. Very little about Esther has been passed down. In the *shtetl,* and in the stories they told us in America, they were Itzak *stolyar's kinder,* Isaac the carpenter's children.

The sisters were all strong women. They seemed to have taken their father as their role model, not their mother. On the other hand, they cooked and baked and were *balabustas* (Yiddish, women in charge, talented homemakers) as well as overpowering, often domineering, mothers and wives.

All six of Itzak and Esther's daughters immigrated to America. In America, their husbands woke at 4 AM to go to the wholesale market to buy products for their corner stores in poor city neighborhoods in which they eked out a living in the 1920's and 1930's. Only Inda, who accepted her cousin Sam's proposal and came to America alone when she was 17, did not live "behind the store." Sam, who grew up in Heisin and probably learned his craft there, was a cutter in a clothing factory. He and Inda and their children lived in a row house within walking distance of the sisters and their stores.

When there was a little extra money, the sisters and their husbands went to the Yiddish theater, often together. They bought records of the great cantors from Europe singing "*Eli, Eli*" and "*Kol Nidre*" and played them on the Victrola in the parlor behind the store. They bought the recordings of Molly Picon and Menasha Scolnick, stars of the Yiddish theater.

At weddings and bar mitzvah parties, they danced to *klezmer* music and Russian *shers*, the women seductively dancing with each other or their men, the women who always dominated the dance floor. Even when they visited each other, they often broke into a *freilich*, a circle dance to Yiddish folk music, in the living room behind the candy store or grocery store of whichever sister's home they were in. The floor shook from their heft and their enthusiasm, and we, the American born children and grandchildren, knew that so long as these strong women were with us, nobody could hurt us.

They were said to have been beautiful young girls, and that's the way they thought of themselves, each of them, till the day they died.

"*Itzak stolyar's kinder zonen alleh shain.*" All of Itzak *stolyar's* children are beautiful.

This was the response whenever any of their children or grandchildren or great grandchildren was complimented. This was, they told us, what the townspeople in Sobolifka had said about them when they were growing up.

In the years of my childhood, they were strong, overweight women in orthopedic shoes. They wore corsets with whalebones to support their matronly figures. Those extra pounds were not a burden to them. They were symbols of prosperity.

Their men were mostly silent shadows.

Malka and Goddel — A Love Match

Malka and Goddel Sapoznik, my grandparents, were 17 and 18 when they married in the first years of the 20th century. While my grandmother never told me she was the older one, it was whispered by others in the family that the bubble was a year or so older than the zayda. Though theirs was an arranged marriage, it was also a love match. More than half a century after his death, she told me she still remembered his touch.

Only one photo of Goddel has survived. In it, he stands proudly like a Russian warrior in the uniform of the Czar's army, silver epaulets on his shoulders, and a gleaming emblem on his cap. The cap looks as if it is made of Persian lamb, and complements his short hair. The photograph was taken during the Russo-Japanese War, about 1905, when he was drafted into the Czar's army because the army needed tailors to make military uniforms. My grandparents were already parents of two children.

Goddel in the Czar's army.

Though I never knew him, I know this face. It is the face of my Uncle Lou, his son. There was much of him in the faces of his daughters, but looking at this photo is like looking at my Uncle Lou. I know, though I can barely see it, that under his cap is that tightly curled, reddish brown hair that Lou had before he turned gray. The wide flourish of Goddel's mustache does not hide the thin, disciplined line of his upper lip. I know that mouth. I have seen it open in laughter. I remember the feel of it on my toddler cheek. It is not his mouth that I know. It is not his mouth that I feel. It is the mouth of his son, my uncle.

Goddel died in the *shtetl*. He lived, however, in the stories his widow and children told us.

He came from the town of Kiblich, nine miles southwest of Sobolifka, two hours from my bubbe's home by horse and wagon. My grandmother remembered stealing a look at him when the families came together to talk about their children marrying. He was handsome, she said. She liked him.

Though my grandmother was a true daughter of the *shtetl*, she was fortunate enough to have a father who valued his daughters. Before he arranged a marriage of one of his daughters, Itzak asked his daughter if she wanted to marry the young man. This wasn't the case in every family, even in my own father's family.

My father, unlike my mother, did not share the memories of his childhood in Europe with me. But one summer afternoon, long after my mother died, when he was sick and old and lonely, he and I sat on my patio enjoying the day.

His father, Nathan Ladiszinsky, arrived in America in 1913 with his brothers and sisters and his aged mother. He left his wife Maryam and four little boys, including my father, in the care of his wife's brother in the town of Sorocco, in Moldavia. It was not unusual for men to leave their families in Europe. Usually, they sent for them as soon as they had work, as soon as they saved the money for steamship tickets. It took my grandfather Nathan seven years to save enough money for five tickets. (The surname, "Ladiszinsky," was Americanized to "Litz," probably at Ellis Island, when Nathan and his siblings and mother went through Customs.)

This is the story my father, Samuel Litz, told me that sunny day on my patio.

"In the house there was a girl cousin. She was older than I was, but still a child. We were friends. Maybe she was 16 when her father, my uncle, arranged a marriage for her. The man she was to marry was a widower, an older man, with children.

"My cousin didn't want to marry this man. She came to my bed and hid under the covers so that they could not take her to the *chuppa* (marriage canopy). They found her and dragged her to the *chuppa*.

"After the wedding ceremony, she hid again in my bed. Of course, they found her and took her to the marriage bed. She came to my bed again and again, and each time they found her and took her back to her husband.

"Soon, she was pregnant, and soon she had a baby. It wasn't long before she had another baby.

"Then the revolution came, and she took her two children and disappeared into the revolution."

A shudder went through my body at my father's words. I pictured this young girl choosing to be a camp follower rather than accept the life she had been forced into —by her own father.

Malka and Goddel, my grandparents, were married in Sobolifka, and moved into a small house next door to Itzak and Esther, Malka's parents. It was a house Itzak *stolyar* built for his children.

In this house the young couple started their family of six children, four daughters and two sons. Later, Goddel bought a larger house higher on the hill to accommodate the growing family. It is possible that Itzak and other carpenters who worked with him also built the second house.

Though there are no records to check, because of a fire in the building which housed records of the area, my grandparents probably married toward the end of 1902. My grandparents' first child, Frayda, was born in September, 1903.

Their second daughter, Chaika, was born in 1905, then Labe, a son, in 1907. My mother, Fayga, was born in October, 1909, and the youngest child, Somela, in 1912.[2] One of their baby girls, whose name is lost to us, died of diphtheria when she was about two years old. The baby girl who died was the last born, probably in 1913 or 1914. Malka's little girl and her youngest sister, Frima's, little boy died during the same epidemic. "They walked hand in hand always," my grandmother told me, "and they died together."

My grandfather, Goddel, was a *schneider,* a tailor, but he was more than that. He was a designer, according to his children.

He worked for a wealthy Polish family who owned a sugar processing plant. Sugar processing has been a major industry in southwestern Ukraine, particularly in the province of Podolia, for generations, and sugar processing and packaging continues today in that region.

My grandfather, in his position as a resident designer and dressmaker to a wealthy family, had one foot in the world of the centuries-old Russian Empire, and the other foot in the world of French couture.

Every Monday morning, Goddel got on his beautiful white horse, which belonged to his employers, and rode to his employers' large estate. Friday, he came home to his family before the Sabbath.

Twice a year, his employers sent him to the Paris fashion shows. There, he took note of the new fashions,

2 The Yiddish and English names of Malka's children are used interchangeably throughout this book. The names are: Frayda (Frayda); Chaika (Ida); Labe (Lou); Fayga (Florence); and Somela (Sol, later Charles).

purchased the necessary velvets and silks and wool, the fine trimmings, and returned to the Ukraine and to the estate of his employers.

It was his responsibility, and that of the other tailors he hired, to ensure that the women of the Polish factory owner's family were dressed in the latest Paris fashions, that their children were dressed as the privileged children they were.

And always, my grandfather purchased extra fabric. There was enough left over to make Malka beautiful designer clothes, and pieces here and there from which he made a little girl's holiday dress, a fine shirt for a little boy. Whatever was the latest style, the hats, the suits, the coats, Malka wore.

Malka and Goddel's children, dressed in their holiday finery, about 1912.

Every Sunday evening, the night before he left for the Polish factory owner's estate, Goddel shined his children's shoes, and lined up all the perfectly polished shoes on the window sill.

Malka and the children were not alone during the week. Itzak and Esther, her parents, lived next door. Though her older sisters had already left for America, there were younger sisters and a baby brother and lifelong friends and the pattern of generations of Jewish life.

Still, the fact that her husband was away all week had to be one of the reasons she became the strong, outspoken woman her family remembers, the matriarch who overcame young widowhood and led her children out of the dangers of war and revolution.

She once told me a story of the early days of her marriage that gave me a glimpse into Malka, the young woman.

It was an evening when Goddel was home. He was playing cards with his *chaverim* (his friends). At a break between card games, Malka brought tea and cake to the table. She walked around the table, offering refreshments to the men. When she reached her husband, he motioned her away with his hand.

It was her time of the month, and in the world in which she lived, when a woman was menstruating, she had to be completely separate from her husband. There was no touching, not sexual, not even the accidental touching as she brushed a hand against his arm when she offered him a plate of cookies.

When the men finished their game and left Malka and Goddel's home, she turned to him in anger and said, *"Hare zech an, mine mon, don cheverta doff nit vissen ven ich hub mine tzite."* (Listen to me, my husband, your friends do not need to know when it is my time of the month. From this moment on, I will serve you when I have my period.)

And, she told me, from that day on, *"Tzis geven azoy."* (That's the way it was.)

According to the ritual laws of purity, a Jewish husband and wife were not permitted to touch each other when the woman was menstruating, and for several days after that. A menstruating woman was considered unclean. Sexual relations between husband and wife were forbidden until she went to the *mikvah*, the ritual bath, a week after her period ended. The same law applied after childbirth.

Today, all women who practice Orthodox Judaism, and many who consider themselves Conservative Jews, follow these ritual laws. In my grandmother's time in the *shtetl*, there were few women who did not. It is likely that my grandmother went to the *mikvah* after her period and after childbirth. However, she apparently drew a line between sexual contact and the nonsexual contact between a wife and husband she described to me. Also, she had a sense of privacy and pride. Her husband's friends did not need to know when she was menstruating.

In the book, *The Memoirs of Gluckel of Hamelin*[3], Gluckel of Hamelin, who lived in the 17th century, wrote the following about the final moments of her husband's life:

"Whereat I said to my husband, 'Dearest heart, shall I embrace you—I am unclean?' For I was then at a time I dared not touch him. And he said, 'God forbid, my child—it will not be long before you take your cleansing.' But, alas, it was then too late."

I imagine my grandparents during the early years of their marriage, filling their home with children, living the traditional *shtetl* life at a time when young Jewish men and women in other towns— and perhaps in their own town — were beginning to imagine a world without a Czar. Young Jewish men and women left the *shtetl* to work in factories

3 Marvin Lowenthal, trans., *The Memoirs of Gluckel of Hamelin* (New York: Schocken Books Inc.,1977), 150-151.

in big cities. Others left their families forever and crossed the ocean to America. In neighboring towns, Kamenitz, Heisin, and others, Zionist idealists dreamed of a life in the ancient land of Israel. They marched next to Socialist idealists who dreamed of a Russia where the peasant and Jew would honor each other and work together to build a new society, a society without a Czar.

Did my young grandparents see that their world was changing? Does anyone living in a time of revolutionary change see the dangers ahead?

And how did my grandmother feel, as each of her sisters left for America, until she was the last child of Itzak and Esther in the *shtetl*?

For hours that day, I sat with Malka at her kitchen table, the tape recorder between us, my notebook in front of me. In between our laughter and her tears, I filled myself with her stories, as well as her food.

The Sisters' Stories
When it Rained on the Bride and Groom

As I listened, my grandmother continued with another story about life in the *shtetl.*

"Inda and Yetta (two of her younger sisters) were young girls. I was already a mother. I don't remember if I had only Frayda or Frayda and Chaika, and by us in the *shtetl* the *chuppa* was ripped. (*Chuppa* is Yiddish and Hebrew for the canopy under which the bride and groom marry. The *chuppa* is a symbol of the Jewish home the couple will create.)

"We kept the *chuppa* in the *shul* (the synagogue). All the weddings took place in the *yarid*, the center of town where the market was when it was market day. Thursday was market day in Sobolifka.

"When there was a wedding, and that was never on market day, the men carried the *chuppa* into the center of the square, and everyone came outside to the wedding. If, during the ceremony, it began to rain, *hut g'pished oif di chusin un di kalla* (it peed, i.e. rained, on the groom and bride) since the *chuppa* was ripped.

"My sister, Inda, had a *kepeleh* (a good brain, she was a bright girl). She thought of and did things that the other sisters didn't think of. So, Inda said to Yetta, '*Her zach ayn, Yetta,*' (listen to me, Yetta) and they were both very good with a needle and thread, and she said to Yetta, 'Let's talk to the other unmarried girls in the town, and if every *maidel* (unmarried girl) gives a *kopek* a week (a small amount, perhaps a quarter), we'll have money to make a new *chuppa.*'

"Yetta thought it was a good idea, and my two sisters took on the job of making a new *chuppa*. First they went to all the unmarried girls in the town and everyone agreed to give a *kopek* a week. Now there was one young girl, Moosya..."

Here, my grandmother interrupts her narrative and turns to me. "Maybe you remember Moosya, Sissy, you met her in my house."

Of course, I remembered Moosya. She and my grandmother and her sisters and their husbands played pinochle all the years of my childhood. I knew Moosya, but never, until that moment, had I heard that Moosya was a childhood friend from Sobolifka.

She continued with the story of the *chuppa*.

"Moosya was my age, or older, and she wasn't married. Yet she didn't want to pay like all the other girls. She never gave even one *kopek*."

Inda and Yetta began gathering the small donations, and soon the *kopeks* became *rubles*.

"Even I gave," says my grandmother, and she points out, "I didn't need a new *chuppa*, I was already married.

"The older women helped as much as they could. The men in town, when they had an extra *kopek*, threw a bit of money into the collection so that the young brides and grooms would have a *chuppa* without holes in it. *Gut hot gahelphen* (God helped), and there was money to go to the *yarid* (the market) to pick out fabric, and there was enough to buy material for the Torah cover, too. The Torah cover was also ripped. They began sewing. Inda and Yetta and the other girls came together every week and they sewed for maybe a year. The other girls helped, but Inda and Yetta were the 'artists.' They embroidered Hebrew letters and beautiful flowers and symbols of love on the *chuppa*, and on the Torah cover they embroidered the Hebrew letters, and they did everything so beautifully.

"When they finished their work, Inda and Yetta told the townspeople that the new *chuppa* and Torah cover were finished, and there was a big celebration in the town. The celebration was on a Monday, a day when the Torah is read. My father put on his *kapota* (a white, long frock that traditional Jewish men wear on *Yom Kippur*, the holiest day of the year).

"Even though it was a day in the middle of the week, everyone dressed as for the Shabbat and there were four *klezmorim* (klezmer musicians who traveled from town to town and usually played at weddings), and the people came from both sides of the hill, from all the houses of the *shtetl* and all the stores in the *yarid*.

"And we danced and the music played and the men carried the Torah with its new cover through the *yarid* and the people followed the Torah into the *shul*. Then they carried the new *chuppa* through the town and into the *shul*, and we all danced and clapped and were so happy. The *maidlech* (young girls, unmarried girls) were hugging each other because they knew that when they stood under the *chuppa,* even if in a storm, there would be no more soaked brides and grooms in Sobolifka.

"And what should I tell you, Sissy? Guess who was the first one to be married under the new *chuppa*? This Moosya, who didn't want to give even a penny! Honest to God!

"Years later, I said to her, 'Do you remember that you didn't give even a *kopek* for the *chuppa* and you were the first one married under it?' And she said, 'I didn't have a penny to give.'

"She was a smart one," my grandmother confides, of Moosya, "and we were friends all our lives. She lived two blocks from me. And she came to me every Saturday. When she died, her son didn't even let me know. We were children together in Sobolifka. I wasn't at Moosya's funeral because her son, that *paskunak* (nasty person), showed me such disrespect. He did not call me to tell me his mother, the friend of my childhood, had died!"

Inda Goes to America

There is no record of how many brides and grooms were married under the *chuppa* made by the young girls of Sobolifka. Inda, the sister with the *kepala* and the imagination to do something about the torn *chuppa,* was not one of them. She was married under a *chuppa* in Baltimore, Maryland, in 1908.

One day, the family in Sobolifka got a letter from Itzak's cousin, Samuel Grossman. Sam had gone to America a few years earlier, and settled in Philadelphia. He wrote that he had a good job as a cutter in a clothing factory, and it was time for him to marry.

In the letter, Sam asked Itzak if his daughter, Inda, would come to Philadelphia to marry him. "I'll go," she told her parents. Though they were cousins, not sweethearts, Inda, the young girl with a *kepala* (a good brain), was adventurous enough to cross the Atlantic Ocean without her parents to start a new life with a young man she knew only as a relative. She wrote a letter to Sam accepting his proposal, and he sent her a ticket to the Golden Land, America.

Inda said goodbye to her parents and sisters and the friends with whom she had sewn the *chuppa*.

She was 18 years old when she arrived at the Port of Philadelphia on January 13, 1908, on the ship, The Haverford. Her immigration record shows her destination was Baltimore. Though Sam Grossman had sent for her, she went directly to Baltimore where her two oldest sisters had settled. A few weeks later, Inda and Sam were married in Baltimore.

Yetta, Inda's sewing and embroidering partner, was married under the *chuppa* made by the young girls of Sobolifka. But her marriage brought heartbreak, not happiness.

Yetta—Marriage and Divorce

"My sister, Yetta, was a young girl, though not yet marriageable age. I was already married and had my first child. My father hired a young man, Shepsal, as his apprentice. Shepsal was from another *shtetl*. He had only a mother. His father was dead.

"You could see that Yetta and Shepsal liked each other. First they were just children, nothing to worry about. But as time went on, they began *shpielen*."

Though the word translates to "playing," my grandmother explained that they were always "looking for places to hide."

"Shepsal asked my father if he and Yetta could marry. My father liked Shepsal. He was a good worker. Shepsal's mother came to Sobolifka to meet us and the two families agreed that their children would marry.

"A half year later, it was a *yom tov* (a holiday). I don't remember which *yom tov*. Shepsal's family came to take Yetta to their house for a visit. When she came to their town with Shepsal, she saw that the grandfather, her future mother–in–law's father, was sitting outside on a step, barefoot.

"We had not seen this. We did not live like this. We had a house on the hill above the market. It was *a shayneh shteib* (a fine house)."

In the *shtetl* of Sobolifka, as in all *shtetlech*, the houses surrounded the marketplace and continued high above the marketplace. More prosperous families lived in the homes on the hill. The poorer families lived in small, bare homes close to the marketplace, the *yarid*. Itzak and Esther's home was high on the hill above the market.

Also, there were poorer *shtetlech* and more prosperous ones. Shepsal's town was a poor town. Yetta realized that she was marrying well below her expectations, and even in the *shtetl*, love did not conquer all.

As my grandmother explained, "Yetta took a look and when she came home, she tore up the marriage contract and put it in an envelope and sent it back.

"A few years later, another *chusin* (prospective husband) came. Another contract was signed. And this too was not good. *Nit g'taghed, vidur nit g'taghed.*" (It was not good, and again it was not good.)

There were several suitors, and none suitable.

"She was already 22. By us, this was an old maid. I was married at 18. So this man came. He came from another town, Bershad, also in Podolia Gubernia."

He was referred by their father's good friend, who lived in Bershad. This *gita bruder* (good brother, friend who was like a brother) suggested that this would be a good match for Yetta.

"I was sitting with my mother and father when this man came. I interrupted and said we should go first to see the family, to see who they were, because I knew that my sister, Yetta, had already had bad luck. This man, who was a friend of my father's friend, not someone we knew, said, 'Look at her, this child, she thinks she knows of such things.'

"So I had to be quiet," my grandmother says. "My mother was also quiet. Only the two men spoke. This was the way it was in Sobolifka.

"Our father wanted Yetta to get married. She was getting too old and there had been too many suitors.

"That Wednesday, the man from Bershad who had suggested the match brought the *chusin* (bridegroom — here, my grandmother means "prospective bridegroom") and his family to Sobolifka. The *machetunim* (the prospective groom's family) came with presents. They were wealthy. They were fur dealers, not just furriers. They had a big plant, and they had a bakery, too. They had a maid in the house and they had two cows. The young man had no father, only a mother and a brother-in-law who ran the business."

After the meeting of the two families, Itzak asked his wife, Esther, "*Nu*, what do you think?"

Here, Bubbe interrupts her narrative to tell me what a fine man Itzak was, what a handsome man, with a fine beard. "Oh, what a pity that I have no pictures. Whenever

I think of it, it gives me pain. Not one photograph! And he was very *frum*, too" (religious, observant Jew).

The *chusin's* family wanted a wedding right away. It was before *Pesach* (Passover). They broke the plate and made the *shidach* (the match). Now, there was an official engagement, a legal contract according to Jewish law.

"The mother–in–law didn't know what to do for Yetta, she was so nice. But the *chusin* didn't talk much. I noticed, and I didn't like it, and I said to Goddel, 'Why doesn't he talk?'

"He, the *chusin*, wasn't ugly. He was presentable, but I thought you could see something was not right. When he came to us for *Pesach*, he didn't want to go home. He said, 'Let's have the wedding now.'

"My father made a beautiful wedding, and Yetta was married under the *chuppa* she had made with our sister, Inda. The *chusin* wanted to go to his home and his town right after the wedding, so Yetta went with him and his family. The family fixed up a nice room for them in their house in Bershad.

"She lived with her husband for a few months as his wife."

Here, I interrupt and tell her that I had heard that Yetta ran away on her wedding night.

"*Nisht emis*" (Not true), my bubbe says. "She lived with him a few months."

I insist that my mother and her sister, Ida, told me that Yetta ran away the first night.

"They were not there," my grandmother says. "I was already a mother of three children and I knew what was happening."

I responded that I was a mother of three children, and she could speak plainly to me.

She explained that, at night, when the newlyweds were in bed together, he suffered what was probably epileptic

43

seizures at a time when it was not only frightening, but there was no treatment. One market day in Bershad, Yetta recognized some of the peasants who either lived near the *shtetl* of Sobolifka, or came to the market in Sobolifka.

She ran to one of the peasants she knew and started to cry. He asked her what was wrong, and she said she wanted to go home. He took her, "*naket and borvis*" (naked and barefoot.) In other words, without anything but the clothes she was wearing. Her husband's family had given her many valuable gifts, and she left them all.

When she came home, her mother and father were frightened.

My bubbe tells me the story as if it happened yesterday.

"Yetta told them the *tsuris* (troubles), and she cried. She was their child. What should a mother and father do?"

The mother–in–law came and swore she had never seen her son in a seizure. She talked Yetta into staying with her husband, continuing to live with him. But Itzak refused to send his daughter back to the mother–in–law's home in Bershad. The two families agreed the young couple would stay in Sobolifka. Yetta would live with her husband in a house behind her parents' home, with a yard between the two houses.

My bubbe continues, "It was a *Shabbos* (Saturday, the Sabbath) afternoon. We used to sit outside with our children on a *Shabbos* afternoon. Labele, my baby boy, was on my lap. We were sitting in front of the house.

"A neighbor heard screaming from Yetta's house. We didn't hear it because there were long rooms and a yard between the two houses. My father and mother and the neighbors started running. Yetta had gone to the cellar to get something, and her husband fell on her. He couldn't get up and neither could she. She was like a dead one. The men were able to lift him, and she was saved."

This time, Yetta would not go back to the home she shared with her husband, even though the home was near her parents' home. Her father and Goddel stayed with the son–in–law all night and Yetta stayed with Malka. By now, the couple had been married more than a year.

In the morning, Itzak sent a telegram to the *machetanesta* in Bershad, and she quickly came with her son–in–law.

"Again she lied and said she had never seen him do this" my grandmother said.

Yetta relented one more time. She knew it would not be easy for her as a divorced woman. Itzak made his son–in–law a foreman in his shop. They continued to live in the house behind Itzak and Esther.

Not long after that, Yetta's husband fell into a seizure in Itzak's shop. This time, Itzak saw it with his own eyes. The mother came again, and took her son home without his wife. She brought with her all the jewelry and furs and household gifts she and her family had given Yetta when the couple married.

Yetta's husband didn't want to give her a divorce. And under Jewish law, the husband has to actually place the divorce papers in his wife's hands to free her from the marriage vows. Without a *get*, a divorce according to Jewish religious law, Yetta would be tied to this man whether or not they ever lived together again. She would be an *aguna*, a woman considered married, still wife to the man she did not live with.

The two families argued. They went to the rabbis for help, and there came a day when Yetta's husband, whose name has been lost to family history, agreed to give her a divorce. The rabbis worked out the conditions of the *get*. Yetta would bring to the divorce proceedings every piece of jewelry and everything else of value that were marriage gifts, and turn them over to the rabbis. The rabbis would give the valuables to the husband after he handed his wife the papers that would free her. But when Yetta came to the *Bet Din* (the rabbinical court) with her jewels and furs and household gifts and put them in the hands of the rabbis, her husband refused to give his wife the *get.*

My bubbe, as she tells me the story, is transported to the past. "My poor Yetta. What would become of her?"

Even in the *shtetl*, in the early part of the 20th century, there were ways around the law.

"Your grandfather Goddel's oldest sister was a widow," she explains. "Goddel went to see her. Maybe my father went also—I don't remember. This widow lived in the same town as Yetta's husband and his family, Bershad. This was the town where they had to get the divorce.

"The widow tricked Yetta's husband into giving her the *get.* She brought a beautiful young girl to him, and said, 'Why do you want Yetta? Here is this young woman, and she has money, too. Give Yetta the *get* and this woman will marry you.' This was not true, but the husband believed her.

"God helped, and after three days, he gave Yetta the divorce."

The old lady and I had been sitting in her kitchen for hours. The afternoon sun had disappeared, and still she talked, and still I wrote. She was transported to the past, reliving the days of her youth. Sometimes she was near tears. I worried that I was tiring her with my questions. It was time for me to go home. At the same time, I didn't want to leave. Who knew if there would be another moment like this for the two of us?

The loving granddaughter won out over the writer. "Bubbe," I suggested, "Shall we stop now? Why don't you take a nap, and I'll come back another day?"

"No, no," she insisted, as she got up to put the teapot on. "We'll eat a little, and I will tell you more."

Goddel in the Czar's Army, and a Public Kiss
In My Grandmother's Voice

"My mother was blind. My father was old. And my husband was in the army. As soon as Yetta came home, they took Goddel for a soldier. I already had two children, Frayda and Chaika.

"They drafted Goddel because they needed tailors to make uniforms for the soldiers. It was already *malchuma* (war — in this case, it was the Russo-Japanese War).

"Yetta and I became 'business ladies' in the *yarid* (the weekly market in the *shtetl*). What did we know? We had only been to the market as customers, not as business ladies.

"They gave Goddel a billet for a year, and they sent him home after the year. Then they took him for another year. My father said to me, 'Daughter mine, whatever money you have, give it to me, and I will go to the army where Goddel is and get him out with the money.' I had maybe 150 rubles, and I gave it to him.

"With the money I gave him, my father went to where Goddel was and *hut g'shmeared gelt* (paid a bribe). The authorities then said that Goddel was sick and sent him to a military hospital. He stayed there two weeks. From there, he was supposed to come home.

"And I got no letter. Yetta was already divorced and living with our parents. I was going around like a crazy person because *yom tov* was near and Avromela (diminutive for Abe, her young brother) had no suit to wear. If Goddel had not been in the army, he would have made the suit for Avromela.

"I went to a *schneider* (tailor) who was a friend of Goddel's and I said to him , 'My friend, please help me. If you won't make my brother a new suit, my mother and father will be *meshuga*.'" Though the most common translation is "crazy," here, the Yiddish word, *meshuga,* means "upset." The parents of the little boy were distraught and frustrated because their child, their only boy, had no suit to wear for the Jewish holiday.

"He was a very fine Jew, and a good friend to Goddel, and they used to give each other work at times and he promised he would make the suit.

"It was a Friday night when I went to him. By the time I walked home, the men were walking home from the synagogue. Fraydele saw all the fathers coming from synagogue and her father was not with them and she began to *kveecha* (carry on, scream) and she fell to the floor and all the people coming from *shul* ran into my house.

"Someone said, 'There is a postcard from Sapoznik.' There was another Sapoznik in the *shtetl*, and they took the postcard to him by mistake, so he read it and ran to the *shul* and came with the other men into my house to read me the postcard."

Goddel had written, in Russian, "I am coming home."

"We sat another hour until the train arrived and Goddel came home. My mother ran up to him and hugged him and kissed him. He wanted to give me a kiss and I didn't let him. I had shame before all the people who were still in our house. Honest to God! This I have not forgotten.

"Afterwards, I thought, what have I done? He said to me, 'Look at this! I come home to my wife. My mother–in–law takes me into her embrace, my wife not.'"

So many years later, I know why Malka did not embrace her husband in front of her townspeople. All her life, she was a "lady." She would embrace her husband in a private moment.

Yetta Goes to America

Not long after her divorce, Yetta sent a letter to her sisters in America, and they responded with a steamship ticket. She very quickly went to America.

Bubbe explains, "She had a friend who had married the same month she had. They were like sisters. This friend now had a child and a home and Yetta was a divorced woman in the *shtetl*. She was too unhappy to stay with us. She went to America to start a new life.

"She came to Philadelphia to our sister, Inda. Inda's husband, Sam, worked in a factory where they made men's clothing. He took Yetta with him and asked for a job for her. They hired Yetta. There, she met Moishe, a handsome widower with three small children. It was not long before he was courting her. 'If you would like a nice life, with a good man, marry me,' said Moishe. 'My children need a mother.'"

Yetta went to Baltimore to visit her sisters there. She wanted her older sisters' advice. And she had to decide if she could be a mother to Moishe's three children. Moishe followed her to Baltimore. He endeared himself to her sisters, and promised he would be a good husband to Yetta.

"She wrote me a letter with a photograph in it," my grandmother remembers. "'*Myn tayere shvester* (my dear sister), I have three children just like you.'

"Honest to God! And the photograph was the wedding picture, with Moishe and Yetta and the three children.

"Oy, Sissy, when I tell you these stories ..." says my grandmother. Though she doesn't finish the sentence, I know that she has been transported to days long gone. And that she trusts me to tell these stories, to keep the past alive to the generations to come.

Yetta, Moishe, and his three children.
Wedding photo, in America.

Four — The Good Years Turn to Sorrow and Danger

A Family Trapped

MY GRANDFATHER, GODDEL, DIED TOWARD the end of World War One, in the middle of the Russian Revolution and Civil War. The towns and villages where the Jews and peasants lived were in different hands each week, as one revolutionary army after another took control of the area. The Ukraine was a battlefield. At first, my grandfather continued to get on his horse every Monday to go to the estate of the wealthy Poles who were his employers. But soon, revolution became constant pogrom. The neighboring peasants, who once may have been playmates of the Jewish children, now were revolutionaries, or were taking advantage of the anarchy to steal and rape and kill.

Goddel remained in the *shtetl* to protect, as best he could, my grandmother and their children. He no longer spent his weeks at the estate of his wealthy Polish employers.

One by one, my grandmother's sisters and her brother left for America. Only Frima, my grandmother's youngest

51

sister, remained in the *shtetl* with her little boy, Israel, though her husband had emigrated. Uncle Abe, Frima's husband, was in America several years before Frima escaped revolution and pogroms to join her husband.

When Frima left with her 10 year old son, Israel, my grandmother was the last child of Itzak and Esther in Sobolifka. Itzak was dead. Esther was blind. My grandparents could not leave her blind and helpless mother in the *shtetl*. They were trapped.

Ida, her Father's Daughter and Mother—Daughter Conflicts

I learned more stories about Sobolifka from Malka and Goddel's second child, my Aunt Ida. Ida had the hardest life of all of her siblings who came to America. Despite heart problems and diabetes and the economic struggle of raising four children during the Depression, she lived to be almost 90. She was long retired from her work in a women's clothing factory and living comfortably on her union pension and Social Security when she began to share the stories of the *shtetl* with me. Just as I had taken my tape recorder to my bubbe's house, so, also, did I sit at Ida's kitchen table.

First came the memories of the good years.

"We lived in a big house on the top of the hill in Sobolifka," she told me. "In the front of the house, we had a closed-in porch. Every Saturday night, my mother and father brought our phonograph to the porch and opened the windows, and everyone in town came to listen to the records of the *chazzans* (cantors).

"Sobolifka was a small town. There was a main street, where the *yarid* was, and Thursday was our market day. All around this main street, on every side, were big stores. Behind them were smaller stores, and houses and workshops. The hill got higher as you went behind the main street. Our house was on the hill, next to my grandparents' house. The higher on the hill your house was, the nicer the house. Our house was high on the hill.

"Our house had many rooms. There were three rooms at the back of the house, the kitchen and two other rooms."

Having explained the status of her family in Sobolifka, my aunt moves on to her difficulties with her mother.

"There was a lot of friction between my mother and me, so I spent most of my time with my father or next door, in my grandparents' house.

"My mother didn't raise me," Aunt Ida confides to me, as if she were an American daughter who is not a stranger to family therapy.

"You see," she explains, "Frayda was my mother's first child, and I came two years later. When Louie (Labe) was born, an *ingele,* a boy child, I was also a baby, not two years old. And *hot mir aran gelecked tza de bubbe.* (They sent me to live with my grandmother.)

She insists she even slept in her grandparents' house.

Though the grandparents lived next door, Ida, a small child, felt abandoned by her mother, replaced by the boy baby. She is an old woman when she tells me this. So many years later, the discarded little girl hides just under her skin.

"When I got older, I didn't respect my mother. I held it against her that she had sent me out of her home. I was always bitter," she explains.

"As a child, I had eczema. The school authorities wouldn't let me go to school, because of the eczema. My father saw that I didn't get along with my mother and she didn't get along with me and whatever she said, I didn't agree, and whatever I said, she didn't agree, and it was no good in the house.

"I was about seven years old when my father began taking me with him to the estate where he worked all week, and wherever he went, I went with him. I learned to sew and I was good at it.

"Before Christmas and Easter, he had four or five people working with him, designing and sewing new clothing for the family of the wealthy Poles. When he went to the fashion shows in Paris, he took a head tailor with him and he took me, also, because he knew it wasn't going to be good with my mother and me.

"Then, when my father died, I blamed my mother. It wasn't her fault."

Pogroms, War and Revolution—the Terrible Days

From the time my grandfather Goddel was drafted into the Czar's army during the Russo-Japanese War until the Soviet Revolution ended, the battle lines of one war after another passed through the towns and villages where the Jews lived. During the years of Imperial Russia's participation in World War One, 1914 to 1917, about 80,000 Russian Jews, most from the Ukraine, were drafted into the Czar's Army, taken from their homes and their families to the front, the next town or village, where the fighting continued.

In February, 1917, with the success of the Soviet Revolution, the new government of Russia walked away from its country's participation in World War One to put together the first Soviet government. Most of the Jewish soldiers found their way back to their families, but many young Jews joined the revolutionary movement. They had fallen in love with the idea of equality and comradeship.

Now, for the first time in Eastern European history, the Jews of Russia and the Ukraine, who had been subjects but never citizens of the Czars, would smell the sweetness of citizenship and acceptance. Or so they were told by the dedicated revolutionaries — many of them Jews like themselves.

The hope and elation only lasted a brief few moments, and there is no evidence it ever came to towns like Sobolifka. These small towns continued to be the battlefields when, after the Revolution, the Red Army fought Ukrainian nationalists and other political factions from 1917 to 1923.

No one in my family ever spoke of good days, of the Revolution bringing peace and comradeship. For my grandmother Malka and her children, the worst of times began when the Imperial Russian government was deposed. There would be more blood and violence, murder and rape and hunger and death.

The Cossacks, the Bolsheviks and the Petliura, and the Death of a Beloved Father

"I'll never forget when the Communists came with the pogroms," Aunt Ida tells me, and she is crying again. I know my questions have unleashed hidden memories, moments so frightening that the little girl of the *shtetl* had to bury them in a secret place in her memory, until this moment, when I, with my tape recorder and my questions, uncovered them. Historians may not refer to the Revolution as pogroms, but rather as civil war. To my aunt and the rest of the family, there was little difference.

"*Ven mir delebt nuch a zoine zachin...*"(When you live through such things) "And what we lived through before—when we had the Czar."

Then she adds, "And Frayda lived through more."

"I remember when the pogroms came," Ida says, "with the Kerenskys and the Bolsheviks and the Petliuras — and the Petliuras were the worst. They were not only fighting each other. They were killing everyone.

"They came into the town and they went after the young girls. Once my father ran with me and hid me in the oven where they made bread. He told me to be still. To be quiet. *'Shvag!'* I was still a child, not a teenager, but I was pretty and round and he knew I was in danger.

"The Cossacks weren't as bad as the Petliuras," she says. "The Bolsheviks weren't as bad as the Petliuras." And I, in my ignorance, ask, "Who were the Petliuras?"

She looks at me as if I were an illiterate child. "You never heard of the Petliuras?"

The Petliuras were the followers of the Ukrainian leader, Symon Petliura, who led the movement for Ukrainian independence. He and his followers wanted to break away from centuries of Russian dominance, and the revolution gave them the opportunity to do so. They fought the Bolsheviks on the battlefield, which happened to be every town in the Ukraine. The followers of Symon Petliura have been held responsible for many of the most vicious pogroms of this violent period.

In 1926, Symon Petliura was assassinated in Paris by Simon Schwartzbard, a Ukrainian Jew who lost 15 relatives in a pogrom. Schwartzbard, who was tried in a Paris court, was acquitted of the crime after his attorney told the story of the Petliura massacres.

It was the Petliuras who came into the synagogue in Sobolifka that terrible night and forced the worshipers to dig their own graves. It was the Petliuras who sent my grandfather on his life or death mission to save his fellow worshippers. "Go to every house," they told him. "Bring us all the gold and silver and money that the Jews have, and if these men are still alive when you return, and if you bring us enough gold and silver, we may let them live."

But the Petliuras were not the only murderers.

My aunt continues, "There were Jewish murderers, too. They were on the side of the Revolution. They weren't from our *shtetl*. They got used to killing, just as their comrades did."

Now, Ida is back in the nightmare of the revolution. I can't direct her to my questions. The words are coming from her mouth so quickly, one long sentence after another, as if my questions have unleashed memories she suppressed for a whole lifetime.

She tells me about the rape of a beautiful woman in the *shtetl*. "They raped her, many of them raped her, and then they killed her."

Through her tears, she tells me of pogrom after pogrom during the post revolution chaos. Once, when the murderers came riding into the town, her father gathered his older children, Frayda, Ida, Labe, and Fayga, and directed them to hide, "And when they leave," he told them, "whoever is alive will come out."

"And we ran to the *barg* (hill) because there were *shteibele* (small houses) there."

My mother, Fayga, was about six. Her brother Labele , perhaps eight. Ida, closer to 11, and Frayda, 13.

I asked, "Were you all together or were you separated?"

"Who could go together?" was Ida's response.

"Once, we hid in a house that had a long hallway. We hid in the hallway. There were others with us. One of those with us was this handsome young man. Maybe he was 17 or 18. I don't remember his name. I liked him. You would say I had a crush on him. And a teacher was with us, too.

"We were all together and the Petliuras came in. The teacher and the Petliuras spoke nicely to each other, and we heard them say to the teacher, in polite language, 'Don't worry, we're not going to hurt anyone.'

"Then, they took about ten young men outside — *kinder* (children), young people only a few years older than we were — and they killed them. And one of those they killed was the young man I liked. For no reason!"

Now, she tells me about a pogrom that lasted three days. "When they left," my aunt says, "We all came out of our hiding places — fathers, mothers, *kinder.*"

My aunt seems to have forgotten her English. Every word she speaks is in Yiddish, the language of her childhood. She is a child again, a terrified child.

"I was hiding with Labele. Somela and Faygele were with our mother and father. Frayda was hiding somewhere else, not with the family. The pogrom lasted for three days. Labe and I got separated.

"When the Petliuras left, everyone was afraid to come out of the hiding places. We waited a whole day. Faygela was sure we were dead, and I was sure she was dead.

"Labela was the first one out. He walked out of the cemetery. I asked, 'Labela where were you?' He was hiding under a gravestone in the cemetery the whole time."

She is back in the *shtetl* as she tells me this story. She has reverted to all the childhood diminutive names of her brothers and sisters, the loving names she had heard so often from her parents and grandparents. Her brother, Lou, is not Labe, but "Little Labe," Labele. My mother, Florence is her little sister, not simply Fayga, but Faygela.

Not all the killers were politically motivated. Neither were they all haters of Jews, she tells me.

"Some of them," my aunt explains, "were neighborhood *shkutzim*, our gentile neighbors. We played together when we were children. But they became hooligans, too. Once, three of them came in to the house where we were hiding. I was lucky. One of them recognized me. He was a friend from our childhood. All three left. Who knows if they found someone they hadn't played with as children? Who knows what they did after they left us?"

The horrors she has repressed for a lifetime are pouring out, one frightening memory after another. Now, she tells me about her blind grandmother. It is a story that is also told by her cousin, Israel.

"Zayda (the grandfather, Itzak *stolyar*) was already dead," she tells me. 'Someone always had to be in the house with the Bubbe Esther. On this day, Fayga and I were with her, and also Frima, and Israel.

"The pogromists were in the town, and the bubbe's house was not a safe place to be because there was no way to get out. There was only one door. It was at the front of the hallway. We were hiding at the back of the hallway.

"It was quiet in the house," she continues, "And from nowhere came three hooligans with their horses. First one came into the house, and then the two others, and they began looking at me. I knew they had rape on their minds. They sent Frima and Israel outside to take care of their horses. They told Frima to make sure the horses were tied to the post, and to give them water.

"Frima, too, knew what was going to happen. She quickly untied the horses and began screaming that the horses were running loose, and the men ran from the house to get their horses.

"She saved me" says my aunt. "But we were never safe. We were only safe for that moment."

Vodka Saves Them

Itzak *stolyar*, Malka's father, had been dead nine months when her husband, Goddel, died. Goddel was saying *kaddish* for him when the Petliuras came into the synagogue and sent Goddel on his life or death mission. Malka lost her father and her husband in less than a year.

My grandmother remembered nothing of the weeks and months after Goddel died. "I don't even know who fed my children," she told me that day as I sat for so many hours at her kitchen table. "I think I had a nervous breakdown."

But now, I am in Ida's kitchen. My Aunt Ida remembers every moment.

"In the *shtetl*, it was the custom to wear mourning clothes for three months. Every day my mother pulled the mourning wig off her head. Every day, she listened for Goddel. For three months! He had taken such good care of her, and of us. Now, in a minute, he was gone. We children were very frightened. It was as if our mother had left us, too. We had to take care of her, as if she was our child. And we were alone in the *shtetl* with the pogroms every day."

Malka tore the mourning wig off her head because she did not accept her widowhood. Her lover, her husband, would soon return to her on his beautiful white horse. She listened for Goddel's steps, Goddel's voice, every day. Her youngest sister, Frima, would soon leave Sobolifka with her son, Israel. Malka could not leave her blind mother alone in the *shtetl*. She and her children were trapped.

There was no one to say *kaddish* for Goddel. His oldest son was too young.

"We had a neighbor," Aunt Ida remembers, "a good friend of my father's, who went to the synagogue every day in rain and snow to say *kaddish* for my father. Even with all the dangers, and after what had happened to my father when he was saying *kaddish* for my grandfather, our neighbor said *kaddish* for his friend, our father. Everybody loved my father."

Eventually, the widowed mother of five children had to "come to herself." The rabbi visited her one day with a few of the other men of the *shtetl*. "Malka," said the rabbi softly, "It is time for you to take care of your children. And we will help you."

The men said they would teach Malka and the children how to run a business. There was a little store on the main street. It was one of the many empty stores left vacant when the Jews of the *shtetl* fled or were murdered during the violence. The rabbi told Malka that the men of the *shtetl* would stock the store for her and the townspeople would buy from her and she and her children would be storekeepers in the *yarid*. There would be money for food on the table for Malka and the children and their blind grandmother.

Malka listened to them. She knew she had no choice.

Ida, as she tells me this, is crying softly. "The neighbors would say, 'There are Goddel's children working.' We had been well off. My mother had a maid all the time."

The store provided a *shtickel laiben,* a meager living, but soon the children and Malka were in another, more lucrative business.

"There were so many soldiers in town all the time. The revolution was fought in all our little towns. And soldiers like vodka," Ida explains.

Malka and the children began making vodka in the bathtub.

We American grandchildren grew up listening and laughing as Uncle Lou and Aunt Ida told us—again and again, their stories of making vodka illegally. Sobolifka was only two hours from the sugar processing plant owned by Goddel's employers, and from the fields of giant sugar beet stalks that grew in the fertile soil. Even if the Polish owners of the factory had fled the revolution, there was still sugar two hours from them, and even in war, there were people processing and selling sugar.

"We went to one town to get sugar, and another town to buy grains," Ida explains. "We needed both to make vodka. We used the grains to bake bread also, so we would not starve. But it was the vodka we sold to the soldiers that put bread on the table for us."

None of the children were going to school. The schools had shut down. Mail from America was not coming through.

When they told us, their American children, those stories, they were funny stories. It was easy to laugh about the terror of a childhood you survived. We laughed with them as we pictured them in the bathtub with the sugar and grains, mixing the ingredients that would become vodka, and when grapes were in season, stomping on the grapes with their bare feet so they could provide wine for the soldiers. We heard story after story of Ida and Lou, the bootleggers of Sobolifka, breadwinners for their family though they were still children.

I wonder, do children get accustomed to war and death, or when they tell these stories so many years later, have they forgotten their terror? I know the answer to the question even as I ask it. When we, their children, were growing up, they told us their stories, but they told them as if they were stand-up comics. They wanted us to know, but not really to know.

Frima's son, Israel, whose harrowing escape with his mother was even more dangerous than that of Malka and her children,[4] remembers that he and the other children walked in the *yarid* on summer nights during the years of violence, spitting out the seeds from the fruit and nuts they were eating, ignoring the bodies of the dead who had been hanged that day. They would *spacheer* (leisurely stroll), he said, enjoying the walk in the town square, while the bodies of young men swayed above them on the telegraph poles. Perhaps they were trying to believe they were living in a more ordinary time, when neighbors listened to phonograph records of the *chazzans* and young girls sewed a new *chuppa* and young couples hid in corners. Spitting out their seeds, not afraid. Or numb with fear and pretending they were safe, as children should be.

Soon, all but one branch of the descendants of Itzak *stolyar* and Esther would be in America.

The Russian Revolution ended in 1921, but the Civil War continued. Still, life went on. Frayda, Goddel and Malka's first child, was 17, marriageable age. There was a young man in the *shtetl* who wanted to marry her. His family came to talk to Malka.

Malka asked her daughter if she wanted this young man. She said yes, she would marry him. For Malka, it would mean one less mouth to feed.

For Frayda, it would mean a lifetime of separation, of facing the bitter truth that she had been abandoned by her own mother.

The day of the wedding, in June, 1921, was also the day of the funeral of Bubbe Esther, the blind grandmother. In the morning, they went to the cemetery and buried the bubbe. In the afternoon, the groom, David Gutnicoff, and his bride, Frayda Sapoznik, stood under the *chuppa* that

4   Israel's first hand account of his escape can be found in Appendix One.

had been made by her aunts, Inda and Yetta, and the other young girls of the *shtetl* in the first years of the 20th century, in a more peaceful time.

FIVE — A MOTHER'S ONLY CHOICE

THE BOLSHEVIKS WERE IN CHARGE in the *shtetl*, and they wielded their power with the viciousness they had perfected during the long years of war and revolution. Though many Jews were socialists and communists, and, indeed, were leaders of the revolution, most Jews in the towns and villages were no better off in the early years of the Communist rule in Russia than they had been during the centuries of Czars and official anti Semitism. And, as the years went by, it got worse.

In the beginning, there was chaos in Sobolifka, as there was in many towns and villages. The new leaders established their socialist state. What was once permitted was now a crime. The peasant had no control over his small piece of land, that meager slice which, under the Czar, had been his. There, he had produced barely enough to feed his family, to enable him to sell the small surplus of his crop at the markets in the neighboring towns and villages. The Jews, who before the revolution, were tradesmen and craftsmen, butchers and bakers, were now told these were capitalistic enterprises. Trying to make a living, to put food on the table for your family, was a crime.

It is likely that Lou and Ida became the bootleggers of Sobolifka when the Bolshevik authorities shut down their little store. They had to find a way to survive, and, as my aunt pointed out, "Soldiers like vodka."

It was against the law to make and sell vodka if it was against the law to sell bread and eggs and fruit in a small store in the *shtetl*, but perhaps the soldiers looked the other way. And children had to be fed, so my grandmother and her neighbors continued to live as they had during war and revolution, avoiding the Bolsheviks, fighting their own war against starvation.

One day, word came to my grandmother that she and her daughter, Ida, and her son, Lou, would soon be arrested. Ida and Lou were the ones who boarded a train to a town two hours away to buy the sugar they needed to make the vodka, and then took another train to the town where they bought the grain, an ingredient in both vodka and bread.

My grandmother and her children had seen enough of the Bolsheviks' justice to know they had to leave immediately.

"When we left Sobolifka," Ida remembered, "we ran away. We didn't even sell the house my grandfather had built for us. It was a nice house!"

I wondered, could they have sold the house if they had more time? In a new form of government called communism? Hadn't the state taken ownership away from the people?

But I realized that they left something more precious than their home in the *shtetl*.

Frayda, Malka's oldest child, and her husband, David, married in 1921. Within a year, Frayda gave birth to her first child, a baby boy, Golya, named for my grandfather and his, Goddel. David had parents and sisters in Sobolifka. The young husband did not want to leave his family. And he pointed out that his infant son, Malka's first grandchild, could give them all away as they stole across borders illegally. Babies cried. There were stories of guides, even parents, who accidentally smothered wailing infants by clasping a hand over the child's mouth to keep the group from being discovered.

The young husband promised his mother–in–law that he would follow her to America when the child grew older.

Years later, my grandmother insisted she would not have left the *shtetl* if she had known that Frayda and her family would be lost to her. More years later, my grandmother long dead, I sat at a kitchen table in Kiryat Yam, Israel, at midnight with my Aunt Frayda and her daughter, Zena, and listened as my cousin Zena shared another version of the story. Our grandmother had pressed her daughter to leave with her, Zena said. "Leave your husband here if he doesn't want to come with us," she told her daughter. "I will take you and the baby. In America, we will say you are a widow. You will start a new life."

But Frayda could not do that. He was a good man. They were husband and wife.

That night, at the kitchen table, Frayda told me that all her life, when David's sisters wanted to hurt her, they reminded her that her mother had abandoned her eldest child by leaving her behind.

SIX — TWO JOURNEYS TO SAFETY

Escape to America

MALKA AND FOUR OF HER children, Chaika, Labe, Fayga, and Somela, began their journey without knowing where it would end.

"Bubbe knew we had to get out of Sobolifka and out of Russia," my Aunt Ida explains. "We didn't have passports. We didn't have money. But the Bolsheviks were after us and we couldn't wait. They would have killed us.

"We left everything, changed what we could into gold, and Bubbe found a guide who took us out of Sobolifka in the middle of the night. We walked all night until we came to a very big city."

The city was Lvov, part of the Austria–Hungarian empire until the end of World War One, and then a Ukrainian city. It was a border city between the Soviet Union and Poland. There was a large Jewish community in Lvov. Their guide took them to the house of a "fine Jewish man with a long white beard." He made arrangements for another guide to take the family across the border into Poland. Their next stop was Shumsk, a smaller city which was then on the Polish side of the border.

They stayed in Shumsk seven months, each child boarding with another Jewish family. The older children worked for their room and board and safety. Malka slept on a cot in a restaurant with Somela, her youngest child. Malka earned their room and board by cooking for the restaurant owner. The family could not be seen together because they had no passports, no exit papers. They would be more noticeable as a group of strangers.

"I went to stay with a *starotsterve,* an official," my aunt says. I interrupt. "Was he Jewish?" She responds, "Of course he was Jewish. The *goyim* (gentiles) would not help us."

Labele was with a roofer. The man had no children and he needed a helper. Labele had never worked as a roofer's assistant in the *shtetl.* He was still a child, a child who had made a promise to his dying father. Labele worked hard, learned quickly. The roofer gave him food to eat and a place to sleep.

A rabbi and his wife took my mother into their home in Shumsk. Fayga was nine years old when the family left the *shtetl.* The only stories she told me about her childhood were stories of hunger and fear. But I knew that the rabbi and *rebbitzen* (the rabbi's wife) were loving to her. Hers was the most pleasant and safest placement. The rabbi and his wife had no children. They treated her as if she were their child. They wanted to keep her.

Aunt Ida, the rounded, pretty teenager, was not so fortunate.

"I milked the cow for the *starotsterve.* Their son was after me, and I had to fight him off many times."

"Were the parents nice to you?" I ask.

She starts to cry. "Were they nice to me? They fed me. My mother used to say, 'What has happened to my children?'"

After a few months in Shumsk, Malka found a scribe who wrote a letter to HIAS, the Hebrew Immigrant Aid Society, which had an office in Warsaw. HIAS, founded in New York in 1881, has a long history of saving Jewish lives by navigating the exit and entry difficulties of a family running from danger toward safety and providing shelter along the way.

"The HIAS knew about us," explains my aunt. "The family in America knew we had left the *shtetl*, because my mother arranged for someone in Sobolifka to write a letter to them. The family got in touch with HIAS in New York, and deposited money for our passage to America."

A Mr. Gold who worked for HIAS was "looking for us," says Ida, and found the family in Shumsk. Though there were thousands of families displaced by World War One and the Russian Revolution, my aunt, when she tells me this, sounds as if she believes that Mr. Gold was searching for one young widow, my grandmother Malka, and her four fatherless children.

There were other HIAS representatives like Mr. Gold all over Eastern Europe. They rescued Jewish families and arranged passage to the United States and other safe havens. It had been their mission since the devastating pogroms in Czarist Russia a century earlier, and would continue to be their mission through World War Two and the immigration of Soviet Jews to the United States and Israel in the 1970's.

Mr. Gold brought my family to Warsaw. There, for the first time since they had left the *shtetl*, they were together. They didn't work. HIAS supported them. Though they lived in one room with five other families, they knew they were now under the protection of one of the Jewish organizations that rescued people like them.

The young widow and four of the fatherless children, taken during the three year journey to America. Left to right: Chaika, Labe, Fayga, Somela, and Malka.

The Doors Almost Close

"Give me your tired and your poor
Your huddled masses yearning to be free
The wretched refuse of your teeming shore
Send these, the homeless, tempest tossed to me
I lift my lamp beside the Golden Door."

Last five lines of the poem, "The New Colossus," by Emma Lazarus, inscribed on the Statue of Liberty in New York Harbor.

When Emma Lazarus, a poet and a Jew, wrote this poem in 1883, she was not part of the "huddled masses waiting to be free." She was an educated and talented American born woman from a wealthy Sephardic Jewish family. In 1883, America welcomed the "huddled masses" of her poem. There were railroad tracks and bridges and city skyscrapers to be built. The men who built them, and their families, wore factory–made clothing and shoes, produced in the factories and sweatshops springing up in big cities and small towns all over the country.

Forty years later, when my grandmother and her children were on their journey, Americans weren't as welcoming as Emma Lazarus had envisioned. They no longer wanted the "wretched refuse of your teeming shore."

Especially, they didn't want the wretched refuse of the Bolshevik Revolution — Eastern Europeans.

The devastation in Europe during World War One, 1914 to 1918, and the Russian Revolution, in 1917, brought hundreds of thousands of refugees to American ports of entry. Many of them were Jews. In the first year of World War One, almost 140,000 Eastern European Jews arrived. They came to relatives who had emigrated before them. They came to save their lives.

But the face of America was changing. There was an anti–immigrant feeling in the country. Soon, changes in immigration law would close the door to families like mine.

The first major change came in 1921. Under The Emergency Quota Act of 1921, also known as the National Origins Act, entry to America was based on the percentage of your countrymen who were already in America according to the 1910 census data. The National Origins Act of 1921 limited the number of immigrants to America each year to 3% of that number.

Then, in 1924, an even more restrictive immigration act was passed. The National Origins Act of 1924 limited immigration to America to 2%, using the census of 1890 instead of the census of 1910. There were precious few

Eastern European Jewish immigrants in the census of 1890 compared to those who came later. Two per cent of their number was negligible.

But unification of families was an exception to the quota, and once again, Mr. Gold of HIAS came to the rescue of my family.

Mr. Gold devised a plan to get the family through the gates of Ellis Island, to circumvent the restrictive American immigration laws. He told my grandmother that her brother, Abe, would claim that she was his mother, not his sister.

Uncle Abe, my grandmother's only brother, was in America, and not married. He was the youngest in the family. He had six older sisters. There was enough of an age gap between Malka and Abe to make Mr. Gold's plan work, with a bit of creativity. Mr. Gold told my grandmother, "Your papers will say that your husband had this son, Abe, from a first marriage, and you, his second wife, raised him. So he is your son. He is in America and he will take responsibility in America for you and your children, who are his sisters and brothers."

After some time in Warsaw, Mr. Gold took my family — and others — to Danzig, a port city on the border between Poland and Germany. Through the centuries, the city was sometimes part of Poland, sometimes a German city, but always, the Jews of Danzig considered themselves German Jews. They identified with the Enlightenment of the 19th century, not with the Hassidic Jews of the towns and small cities where families like mine had lived for generations. These cultured, educated German Jews, like their brothers and sisters in America, helped the ragged, frightened, *shtetl* Jews, but they held their noses even as they came with bags of clothing and boxes of food to the abandoned World War One barracks that Jewish agencies like HIAS took over for refugee housing.

Mr. Gold brought my family to one of those barracks.

"When we got there," my Aunt Ida says, "the authorities would not let us stay. Mr. Gold told us, the younger ones, 'Listen, my children, we will make a commotion, a strike, a demonstration,' and he instructed us to lie down on the train tracks and make noise, and we did."

The authorities relented, and 500 Jewish families under the protection of HIAS were safely housed in an abandoned German army barracks for a full year.

They ate "herring and potatoes" and "herring and potatoes." There were no classes for the children. The people were not permitted to leave the barracks. One by one, as their papers arrived, families left.

Rosh Hashanah, 1923, was my family's turn. HIAS had arranged for religious services in the barracks, and Malka was at Rosh Hashanah services. The children were sitting outside on stoops. They heard the authorities shouting, "Malka Feinstein, Malka Feinstein," and there was Mr. Gold.

My grandmother came running from the barracks, and Mr. Gold told her, "Next week, you and your children are going to America. Your papers have arrived."

HIAS took the family to London in a small ship. When they got to London, the ship they were supposed to board had already left.

"*Oy, Gut,*" exclaims Aunt Ida, as she tells me the story. "We had tickets and we didn't make the ship."

HIAS arranged passage on another, the Majestic, sailing from Southampton.

The night before their ship was to sail, Ida was so nervous as she got her *shmattes* (Yiddish, rags, Ida is describing her clothes) together that she cried all night. In the morning, her eyes were red.

"A Jewish doctor was on the ship. He was the one who examined us all," she remembers. "When he came to me, he said to my mother, 'Mrs. Feinstein, does she have a satchel?' I was sure I was going off the boat because of my eyes. Why else would he want my mother to give him my satchel?

"I started screaming, crying, 'Momma, take the children and go! Leave me here.' I was 15, maybe 16.

"So the doctor said to my mother, in Yiddish, *'Ayrzeck ahn* (Listen) Mrs. Feinstein, you take these three children and board the ship. The ship doesn't leave until 4 o'clock.' Then he said to me, 'Come now with me.'

"He took me to a room and told the nurse to put cold compresses on my eyes and he turned to me and said, 'Don't you cry any more or you will remain here! I believe your eyes are red from crying, but I can't let you on the ship until I'm sure.'

"So I sat and sat, and I didn't cry, and I said to myself, 'I have a sister in Sobolifka. I will find my way back to her.' At three o'clock, the doctor came to examine me, and he said I could get on the ship."

Ellis Island records indicate that they arrived there on November 2, 1923. The passengers on the Majestic stayed on board for three weeks after the ship's arrival.

Yetta and Abe, Malka's sister and brother, were waiting when the ship docked, and sent a welcoming basket of fruit to their sister and her children. Uncle Abe, in the small ferry in the harbor, saw his nephew, Labe, take a banana from the basket, and without peeling it, bite into it. Labe had never seen a banana. Uncle Abe yelled up to his nephew in Yiddish, "Greenhorn, throw away the skin and eat the inside!" (Greenhorn is a derogatory reference to a new immigrant, usually meaning someone fresh off the boat and ignorant.)

Yetta and Abe went back to Philadelphia and returned to Ellis Island several times during those three weeks. But on the day the passengers were able to leave the ship, they were not there.

"We heard someone shouting 'Feinstein, Malka,' It was late afternoon, maybe 4 o'clock," Ida remembers. "We did not know the man who was shouting our mother's name. Even our mother didn't know him. He had come with a small boat to take us to New York. Uncle Abe had arranged this. He was in Philadelphia working.

"We were afraid to get into this small boat with a stranger, and so was our mother. Once we were in the boat, we were afraid he would throw us overboard. He heard us whispering.

"'Don't be stupid,' he said. 'I'm taking you to Philadelphia, but first you have to go to New York.'

"Then Louie said, 'It's America. America is on water.'"

According to my grandmother's immigration records, she was 47 in 1923, when the family arrived. Born in 1883, she was really 40. But in order for her brother, Abe, to claim her as his stepmother, she needed to be older than her actual age. Abe arrived in America in 1914. He was 20 years old. In 1923, when he was 29 years old, it was believable that he had been raised by a stepmother who was 47 years old.

Malka and her children entered America under the name Feinstein, her maiden name. For the rest of their lives, she and her children would remember Goddel and tell their children about him, but they would never carry his name. [5]

---

5 Some of the material in this chapter was first published in the book, "120 HIAS Stories, in commemoration of the 120th anniversary of the Hebrew Immigrant Aid Society. The author's contribution, "A Commotion, a Strike, a Demonstration, appears on 15. The author, Sissy Carpey, holds copyright rights to this story.

Survival in Asia

"I have a sister in Sobolifka and I will find my way back to her," Ida had repeated to herself as if it were a mantra, while the ship's nurse applied cold compresses to her eyes all afternoon, to calm down the inflammation brought on by the young girl's nervous crying while she packed her *shmattes*.

If the ship's doctor had sent Ida off the ship because of her red eyes, and if, by some miracle, Ida had found her way back to Sobolifka, she would not have found her sister there.

Frayda and David, like all the people in the Ukraine, went through famine and fear as the new Soviet Socialist Republic tried to apply the principles of Marxism to the almost feudal economy of the former Russian Empire. Peasants, who had gone to the markets in the town square to sell the fruits and vegetables they had grown on the slice of land which was theirs, were now called capitalists if they sold anything. The new government transformed the peasants' small farms to mega farms, forcing them into faceless agricultural combines, taking them from land on which their families had lived for generations.

The Jews, who were tradesmen and craftsmen, were now told that everything belonged to the people, though the people, Jew and peasant alike, were starving.

The new government, dedicated to the principles of Karl Marx, sold most of the grain from the Ukraine, the bread basket of Russia, to foreign countries so that the USSR had cash to industrialize the Soviet Union. Or they traded grain for industrial equipment. In both cases, there was almost no food for the Russian people.

In October, 1923, when Ida and Malka and the rest of the family boarded the Majestic in Southampton, England, Frayda and David and their baby had already left the *shtetl* to begin their own new life far, far away from the Ukraine, as far east as they could settle and still be within the boundaries of the Soviet Republic.

Somehow, in Sobolifka, David's family learned about opportunities in Central Asia, in a large city, Tashkent, in the province of Uzbekistan. There were Jews in Uzbekistan whose families had been there for a thousand years, descendants of Jewish traders on the medieval Silk Route, and of other early Middle Eastern and Asian traders.

Uzbekistan had been part of the Russian Empire since 1867, when Czar Nicholas II sent troops to invade and conquer the area. Nicholas connected Uzbekistan to the Russian Empire by building the Trans Caucasian Railroad, and now, that railroad would bring desperate and hungry Ashkenazi Jewish families from the towns and cities of the Ukraine to a new world. It was not America. But it might mean life, not death by starvation.

First, David and his mother went to Tashkent. When they returned, they reported that there was work in the big city, that there were Jews there. Most importantly, there was bread. In June, 1923, David and Frayda and their 15 month old baby left the *shtetl* with David's sisters and their husbands and his parents, and took a train across the steppes and mountains of Eurasia, closer to China and Afghanistan than to the Atlantic Ocean that Malka and her children were to cross.

They packed their meager belongings, and left the village that had been their family's home for generations. I picture my young aunt, who only recently had embraced her mother, her sisters and brothers, for the last time, boarding a train with her husband's family to a new world that would take her far away from the life she had known.

There had been no letters from her mother. Malka was leading her four children across one dangerous border after another, finding work and refuge where she could.

When she found a scribe to write a letter for her, it was to the family in America, to tell them where she and her children were in their journey toward them.

A Sacrifice for the Whole Family

It is 72 years later, October, 1995, and I am sitting across from my Aunt Frayda. We are at the kitchen table in my cousin Zena's home in Kiryat Yam, a suburb of Haifa. I had flown to Israel with my notebook and tape recorder to interview the old woman. She had told me on the phone, in the Yiddish which was our common language, "If you want to see me once more, come now."

She was well into her 90's. In the years since her only visit with the family, when the Cold War was ending, I had visited her in Israel several times. Now, her mother, my grandmother, was dead. So, too,were my mother and her sister Ida , and their two brothers, my uncles, Labela and Somela. Only Frayda, who had spent most of her long life in the Soviet Union, still lived. And I needed to interview her, to learn more about her life without us.

But this was not a good time in Israel. My husband wanted to cancel our trip because of a frightening rash of bus bombings in the weeks before we were to go.

When I called my aunt and cousin to tell them we were not coming, my aged aunt responded that her freezer was filled with the knishes and cabbage soup and cookies she and her daughter had prepared for us. More importantly, she let me know how frail she was.

I left my husband at home, and flew to Israel to visit my once lost family.

My cousin Zena and I look like sisters. When she was growing up in Tashkent, her father often told her she looked like my mother, Fayga. When she came to the

United States to visit me for the first time, my daughter, Jodi, gasped, "You didn't tell me she looked so much like you." Zena is six years older than I, a retired pediatrician. Though we did not meet until we were in our middle years, we have always been, from the first moment of our first embrace, as at ease with each other as if we had been children together.

Zena picked me up at Ben Gurion Airport in Tel Aviv, and we drove to her home. It was late when we walked into the apartment. There, sitting on a chair in the living room, waiting for us, was my Aunt Frayda, looking so frail that I knew she had not exaggerated when she said on the phone, "If you want to see me once more, come now."

I am not sure if it was that night, or the next night, the first full day of my visit, that we sat at the kitchen table with the tape recorder between us till midnight, while I furiously wrote in my notebook, in a combination of her Yiddish and my translation.

I may not remember if it was the first night or the second night of my visit, but I do not have to turn to my notebook or the tape cassette to relive those moments.

She sat there, my frail aunt, with the tears running down her railroad-track wrinkled face.

"Ich hot g'vane da kapura far da gontza meshpucha," she said. "I was the sacrifice for the whole family."

"Meir hot gevissed as ven da Bubbe Esther shtarped, meir vet gayen tza da mishpucha in America. Far vus hut mon momma g'mached a shiddach far meir?"

"We knew," she continued, "that as soon as the Bubbe Esther died, we would leave for America. We would be with the whole family in America. Why did my mother marry me off when she knew she was going to leave?"

I tried to respond in Yiddish, to defend my grandmother, her mother.

"Isn't it true, dear aunt," I asked, "that the Bubbe Esther's funeral was in the morning, and you and David were under the marriage canopy in the afternoon of the same day?"

Yes, she nodded. I continued, "And isn't it true that a wedding cannot be postponed?"

She nodded again. Then she repeated. "*Meir hot gevissed meir vet gayen to America.*" "We knew we would leave for America as soon as we could. Why did my mother arrange a marriage for me?"

The author, Sissy Carpey, the lost aunt, Frayda, and her daughter, Zena, a few weeks before Frayda died.

Tashkent—City of Bread

The year 1923, when Malka and her children arrived in America, when Frayda and David and their baby went to Tashkent, was also the year a Soviet writer, Aleksander Neverov, published his most famous book, *Tashkent— City of Bread*.[6]

---

6 Aleksandr Neverov, *Tashkent— City of Bread, published 1923 in the Soviet Union, http://www.sovlit.com/tashkent/*

Tashkent— City of Bread is a Soviet version of *The Adventures of Huckleberry Finn*, by Mark Twain. In both books, young boys survive hunger and become strong.

In Neverov's book, a twelve–year–old boy, Mishka, leaves his village after most of his family dies of hunger. Mishka has heard that there is grain in Tashkent. He decides to go to Tashkent to buy grain. He convinces a friend to go with him.

The two boys make their way to the train to Tashkent. On the train, they see peasants covered with lice, starving people, filth and disease.

His friend dies along the way. At a stop, Mishka finds a potato skin in the mud and eats it. At another stop, he scoops a fish bone out of rubbish in the street and swallows it. The young hero continues to Tashkent. The train stops at Orenberg, and there is another train from Orenberg to Tashkent. He steals on to that train. Hungry, starving, and alone, Mishka reaches the City of Bread. In Tashkent, he sleeps under fences, continues to rummage for food. He gets stronger, finds work, and buys grain.

Some time later, Mishka, tired and dirty, gets off the train at the station near his village. He is carrying two huge sacks of grain. When he returns to his family, he learns that his two brothers have died of hunger. His mother is still alive, though she is near death. When she sees Mishka, she regains her will to live.

The book ends with this sentence: "Mishka decides, 'There's no point in grieving. I'll rebuild it all anew.'"

There was a terrible *imglick* (disaster), my aunt told me that night at her kitchen table in Israel. Strangers came to her, and she gave them grain. In Tashkent there was grain. Everywhere else, the people were starving.

Then she opened her hands and placed her right hand to her shoulder and her left hand at her left foot to show me the size of the huge sacks of grain in Tashkent, the city of bread.

Until 1932, the people were hungry in the countryside. Even after collectivization of the farmland and increased harvests, those who grew the grains were starving. Under Stalin's leadership and the five–year– plans, harvests were sold to other countries or shipped to the industrial cities within the Soviet Union.

SEVEN — IN AMERICA
THE FIRST DAYS

The first photo of the family in Philadelphia— standing left to right, Fayga, Malka, and Chaika; seated, Somela and Labe.

Together at last— left to right, Frima, Yetta, Abe,
Malka, and Inda.

THE MAN WHO WAS A stranger to Malka took them to New York, and then, to Philadelphia by train, and finally, to Yetta and Moishes house in South Philadelphia.

It was very late, past midnight, when the weary travelers walked into Yetta and Moishe's home behind the candy store on the corner of Eleventh and Shunk Street in the immigrant neighborhood of South Philadelphia.

Yetta and Malka, always the closest of sisters, had not seen each other in at least a dozen years.

When they were last together, Malka was the prosperous, pampered wife of Goddel, and the mother of three children. Now, she was a widow who had left her eldest child and her only grandchild in danger in the *shtetl* and had led her four younger children through an Eastern Europe ravaged by war and revolution, and finally, to the ship that had taken them to America. The years had changed Yetta, too.Yetta, when she left the *shtetl*, was a disillusioned, unhappy young woman, unable to make a traditional life as a Jewish wife and mother, marked as a divorced woman. In America, she was surrounded by children who loved her, sisters who lived within walking distance. She was also a business woman, working side by side with her husband in their candy store even as she baked and cooked and mothered her brood of American-born children.

Now, she was the mother of Moishe's sons, Jules and Hymie, his daughter, Leah, and the two daughters she had given birth to, Beatrice and Florence. She loved all five as if she had carried each one in her womb, and there was never a moment that they were not Yetta and Moishe's children, never a moment that they were not loving and devoted sisters and brothers to each other.

Florence, who was always "Fencie" to the family, though I suspect she was named for the same Fayga my mother was named for, was the only one of Yetta's children still alive when I began transcribing my grandmother's tales of the *shtetl*. I couldn't wait to tell her all the details. I called her as I was transcribing. "Fencie," I said, "You won't believe what my grandmother told me. It's all about your mother, and her bad luck with men."

I told her what I had learned about her mother's first romance with a young lover who was too poor, and about her later marriage and divorce. Her mother had shared some of it with her children, but that was nothing compared to my grandmother's openness so many years later. Fencie and I laughed together as we pictured Yetta and her sister, Inda, organizing the young girls of the *shtetl* into a sewing group, crafting a new *chuppa* because the old one had holes in it.

I promised Fencie I would visit her soon and bring her a copy of my transcribed tape.

Fencie, like all the cousins, had always been a part of my life. When I was a little girl and she was a young woman during World War Two, she came to our house after work to freshen up when she had a date during the week. She was a secretary in a defense plant next to the elementary school my brother and I attended. (During World War Two, every American factory, whether it had produced clothing or automobiles, became a defense plant, producing weapons, ships, fighter planes and uniforms, under contract with the United States Government.)

When she married, Fencie and her husband, Harold, rented the middle bedroom in my grandparents' house on Gransback Street, and shared the only bathroom in the house with my grandparents. The young couple had "kitchen privileges," which meant they could fill the refrigerator with their own food and use my grandparents' dishes and pots and pans. But my bubbe cooked dinner every day, and how could she not make enough for Yetta's daughter and her husband? It was an arrangement that worked for the young couple and the loving aunt and uncle.

"I remember the night your grandmother and the children came," Fencie told me. "It was very late, probably past midnight. We knew they were on their way from New York. My father and Uncle Abe had arranged for someone to bring them to our house.

"My brothers and sisters and I were lying awake in our beds, waiting. We were too excited to sleep. When they walked into the house, we jumped out of our beds and lined up on the stairway. Your mother had long braids."

Like many immigrant storekeepers in Philadelphia, Yetta and Moishe and their children lived behind the store. The candy store took up most of the first floor of the building.

Behind it was a small living room and kitchen. There were three bedrooms and one bathroom on the second floor.

My family stayed in that house with Yetta and Moishe and their five children for six months.

Fencie didn't remember where they had all slept. "I guess we all doubled up, slept on the floor," she said.

Her father, Uncle Moishe, was a handsome, authoritative man who was a leader, a patriarch of the family. Years later, when we all gathered in my parents' kosher butcher store on Passover for the family Seder, it was Uncle Moishe, standing at the head of the long aluminum tables, who led the Seder. He had a full head of white hair and a voice like an actor, and we children knew better than to interrupt Uncle Moishe's flow as he went through the Manischevitz Hagaddah.

When he took his wife's sister and her four children into his home behind the store and fed them and kept them for six months, he did not sit still and say *Dayenu.* (During the Passover Seder, a dinner and religious service in which the story of the Jewish people's escape from slavery in Egypt is retold, one of the songs Jews sing is *Dayenu.* There are many verses, and each ends with *Dayenu.* "Had God brought us out of Egypt and not divided the sea for us, *Dayenu.* Had God brought us to Sinai and not given us the Torah, *Dayenu.*"*Dayenu* means "It would have been enough.")

Within a few days of their arrival, Moishe found jobs for Ida and Lou, the two older children. Neither one had any formal schooling. Any education they might have had in peaceful times had been interrupted by war and revolution. Now, they would be breadwinners for the family.

Aunt Ida remembered, "We were only in America a few days when Uncle Moishe found a job for me in a cigar factory.

"The day he told me about the job, he said, 'Tomorrow you'll take the number 23 trolley,' and, of course, he said it in Yiddish, the *drei und tvontzik* trolley, and he took me to the corner where I would wait for the trolley and he also told me where to get off the trolley.

"So the next morning I stood on the corner and began counting the trolleys as they passed. I was waiting for the 23rd trolley."

A conductor, who drove his trolley back and forth on his route, noticed the girl standing on the corner all day. Late in the afternoon, he went to one of the factories on his route and asked the people, "Does someone speak Yiddish here?"

Many people responded that they spoke Yiddish, and he told them, "There is a kid who has been standing on the corner all day. She looks like she's lost."

"Everyone knew I was the new *greena* in the neighborhood," explains my aunt, "so they knew it had to be me. One of the Jewish men in the factory went with the conductor to get me. By the time they came to the corner I had stood at all day, I was crying.

"The Jewish man took me to Uncle Moishe and said, 'Here is your *plemanetza*' (relative). Uncle Moishe responded. *'Greena Touchas!'*" *Touchas* is Yiddish slang for backside. Uncle Moishe was calling Ida an ignorant ass.

The *greena touchas* soon had a group of young friends and money in her pocket.

On the first Saturday of the first week she worked in the cigar factory, she was handed a paycheck. The young people, all immigrants who worked with her, said, "Come with us, Ida. We're going to a Chinese restaurant."

"What did I know about Chinese food?" she asks. "Nothing!"

She went with her new friends, fell in love with Chinese food and America's openness, and "Every Saturday after that I went to the Chinese restaurant with my friends."

Labele, who was about 15 when the family settled in with Yetta and Moishe and their children, soon was working in a butcher shop. Though he spoke not a word of English, and had never cut a piece of raw meat, he walked into a store in one of the many poor neighborhoods of the city, and met a man who would take him under his wing and teach him to be an American breadwinner.

His daughter, Diane, remembers, "My father and this man, Ruby, were friends all their lives. Ruby used to come to our store to say hello to my father every now and then."

At first, my uncle could not communicate with the customers in Ruby's store. It was in a non-Jewish neighborhood. Ruby taught his eager young student how to use the sharp knives to cut and trim the pork chops, the hog's feet, the stewing meat and beef roasts and chickens, how to carve bits of meat from the bones of beef carcasses, to put those bits of beef and fat through the grinder so that Ruby could add them to the ground meat.

My uncle worked in a back room, away from the customers who spoke a different language.

Uncle Lou listened, not only to Ruby, but to the people who came into the store, his American cousins, the sounds of America all around him. He taught himself to read English by reading the daily newspaper, the advertisements on the trolley he took to Ruby's store, the labels on the cans of food, the boxes of noodles and bottles of soda and milk which were in abundance even in the poorer neighborhoods of his new country.

My mother, Fayga, who became Florence in America, was young enough at 13 to go to school. But when she went to the elementary school in the neighborhood with her younger brother, Somela, she was placed with first graders. Though there were enough Yiddish speaking children in the school, and probably more than a few Jewish teachers, there was no special class for children who did not speak or understand English. Soon she stopped going to school. She was self conscious and ashamed at what she saw as her ignorance. No one insisted she go to school. Not her mother, nor her aunts, nor her American cousins.

Somela, who was "Sol" during his first years in America, and later reinvented himself as "Charles," was 11 years old when he walked into his first classroom. He quickly mastered the English language, caught up with the first graders, and was soon an American student with classmates his own age. He was the only one of Malka's children to get even a glimmer of an American education. Though he did not graduate high school, he was the most "American" of Malka's children, and thought of himself as a self educated man.

Uncle Moishe, meanwhile, was looking for an appropriate husband for Malka.

Within six months of their arrival, he told Malka he had found a fine Jewish man, a widower with two children, for her. They married soon after they met, after the six months the family stayed with Moishe and Yetta and their children.

"But it was no good," Ida tells me. "He watched what we children ate, and complained to my mother that 'Your children eat more than mine do.' And he wanted my whole paycheck. I knew most of it had to go to help support the family, but I insisted on keeping some of my money for myself. I was a young girl. I worked hard. I wanted to go to the Chinese restaurant, to buy a new dress. Every Saturday night, the boys and girls would go somewhere— just as teenagers do today. In the summer, my friends and

I went to a concert in the park, and we bought ice cream afterwards."

Generations of Philadelphia's young immigrants and their American born children were introduced to classical music at the summer concerts in the Robin Hood Dell, located in Philadelphia's Fairmount Park. The park, originally laid out by William Penn, meanders through many city neighborhoods, and is as much a resource to Philadelphia and its suburbs today as it was in colonial times, or in the time of my family's first days in America. The Robin Hood Dell is located in Strawberry Mansion, a Jewish immigrant and first generation neighborhood until the 1950's. The Dell was a musical venue that was, and is today, a valley in the park. There was open air seating for paying patrons, and free admission (later a modest fee of a dollar or two) to music lovers who spread out on the grassy hills surrounding the Dell. They brought blankets to lie on and picnic dinners to feast on, and listened to the Philadelphia Orchestra led by its great conductors, with guest soloists who were acclaimed all over the world.

My Aunt Ida was drinking in the sweetness and freedom of American life. Not even for peace in the house would she give that up.

"There were other problems, too" she tells me. "Louie was so close to my mother that he would sit himself down on Momma's bed and talk to her. The husband didn't like that. And the man had a daughter who was our age, and she did nothing. We went to work. She sat on her *touchas* (ass) all day."

Ida told Mema (endearment for aunt) Yetta how unhappy she was, that she was fighting all the time with her new stepfather, that he regularly looked into the refrigerator and kept track of which child ate more than another, that he complained about how much food Malka's children consumed.

Yetta's response was, "Come back here, with us," and Ida left the family and moved into Yetta and Moishe's dwelling behind the candy store. It didn't take long for her brother, Lou, to follow her.

Malka lived with the new husband for a year, a miserable year. Then she told her sisters and her children that she was not staying in the marriage. She would divorce this man, be free of this bad match.

Labele, the son who had promised his dying father that he would always take care of Malka, asked, "Are you doing this for us?" She responded that she did not need to be unhappy with a husband. If she was doing this for her children, she was also doing it for herself. She could not stay with this man. Her son persisted. "Are you sure?" "Avoda," she replied. In both Hebrew and Yiddish, this translates to "the truth." In common usage, it is a way of saying "absolutely," or "without doubt."

EIGHT — AMERICAN COURTSHIPS, AMERICAN LIVES

THE FIRST FEW YEARS IN America went quickly. One day, they were Yiddish speaking "greenhorns," forever scarred by war, revolution, and one pogrom after another. The next day, the two young sisters, Florence and Ida, wore flapper dresses and danced the Charleston.

There were differences between the American born cousins and Malka's children, differences in education, and their expectations of life. In some families, that would have been a barrier to friendship. Not so in the family of Itzak *stolyar* and Esther of Sobolifka, in the Pale of Settlement set aside by Catherine the Great so many generations earlier.

They were the children of sisters, strong, domineering women who wrapped their arms around each other and all that was theirs, even as they argued about the little things in life.

The family settled into an American life. Lou and Ida were the breadwinners. My mother, Florence, took a job in a factory, another in a store. Still a young teenager, struggling with a new language and a new country, she never stayed at a job long.

They never stayed at an address long, either. There is no record of how many tiny row houses or apartments they rented, but whenever we, their children, were with them in those immigrant South Philadelphia neighborhoods, they pointed out this little street and that shabby row house as a place where they had once lived.

Each move may have been a step up. But not much of a step.

Lou and Ida turned over most of their paychecks to their mother, and so did Florence, when she had a paycheck. Malka took their earnings and put so much in an envelope marked "rent," another few dollars in envelopes marked "food" and "gas bill" and "phone bill."

They lived from week to week, and whenever there was extra money in the envelopes, Malka looked for a better place to live.

She had one envelope that her children — or at least her daughters— were not happy about. It was the envelope from which she took a few dollars to attend a charity luncheon or a meeting with her "lady friends," to make a bridal shower for a poor, motherless bride, to do the good deeds the women had been taught by the examples of their mothers and fathers.

Years later, my mother and my aunt were still telling us, with bitterness in their voices, that Malka took money that they, the family, needed, so that she could be seen as a woman of substance.

There is a photo of Malka dressed as if for an afternoon event with the ladies. She is wearing a summer print dress. Her right arm is gracefully and lightly touching a wide doorway decorated with shirred curtains covering its expanse of glass. In her left hand, she is holding a white handbag and white gloves. Under the white hat jauntily placed on her head, her hair is still dark, not gray. It is impossible to tell her age.

Malka, the Society Lady

She is attending one of the ladies' luncheons where she and other immigrant women raised money for others, for those who needed help more than they did.

In her daughters' eyes, she was taking money her children earned so that she could be what they called a "society lady." But I, her granddaughter, remember the bridal showers those "society ladies" made for more than one orphaned young girl, the pennies and quarters they gave to neighbors who needed it. Through those luncheons and afternoon meetings that my mother and aunt considered frivolous, my grandmother stayed true to the values of the *shtetl*. She remained Itzak *stolyar's* daughter and Goddel's wife, a well thought of person in the community who once lived in a house high on the hill. Though she was no longer the prosperous, pampered wife she had been during the peaceful years of her life with Goddel, she had not forgotten what was expected of a Jewish woman.

Young Love in America

My mother, Florence, was the first to marry. She went to a dance of the Heisiner Independent Young Men's Society, and there she met my father.

She was a carefree teenager when she went to that dance. She loved the movies and went every week with her friends. They knew the words to all the songs coming out of Tin Pan Alley. They bought silks and velvets on Fourth Street, a long, narrow street in South Philadelphia that housed one discount fabric store after another. They patronized immigrant dressmakers who, for a few dollars, produced a dress or a suit just like the one the glamorous movie star wore in her latest movie. If there was something to celebrate, a girl turning 16, or a couple getting engaged, their mothers baked and cooked and invited neighbors and relatives into their small parlor.

There were many organizations like the Heisiner Independent Young Men's Society. The *landsmen*, people who had grown up together in the same town in the Old Country, banded together in America, not only to provide business loans, but to provide a social life for each other and for their children. In the open society they found in America, their sons and daughters could befriend — even fall in love with— those who were not Jewish. They wanted their children to marry Jews. To bring Jewish grandchildren into their world. Every weekend there was a dance or a party sponsored by one *verein* or another, where immigrant teenagers met and fell in love and their parents took them down the aisle to a *chuppa*.

It was not the same as it had been in the Old Country. There were few arranged marriages. Still, in that first American generation, each ethnic group stayed with its own. It is true that young Jewish men and women met and fell in love with the Italian and Irish immigrants with whom they worked or made friendships in the free American society. Still, marriage between a Jew and a Gentile was rare. And when it happened, it was usually considered a tragedy for the families.

My father, Samuel Litz, came to America with his mother and three brothers when he was a teenager, in 1920. His father, Nathan, immigrated to America from Heisin seven years earlier, in 1913, with his siblings and an aged mother.

Records of a Philadelphia bank, the Lipshutz/Peoples Bank, indicate that Nathan Litz, my grandfather, deposited $444.25 in American money to that bank in the years from 1913 to 1920. With that money, the bank, working with HIAS, arranged for the family to come to Philadelphia. The $444.25 also included train fare from New York to Philadelphia.

Before my grandfather sent for his family, he bought a small house on a small street in Strawberry Mansion, a Jewish neighborhood just a few short blocks from the Robin Hood Dell. My paternal grandmother lived in that house for the next 50 years, until the last years of her life.

Almost as soon as they got off the boat and were settled in the little house in Strawberry Mansion, someone in the family took my father to a kosher butcher shop, where he became an apprentice. Born in October, 1905, my father was 14 when the family arrived at New York Harbor on May 9, 1920.

He never attended a day in an American school.

When my parents met in that romantic moment my mother described so many times (there she was, sitting on his lap, and she didn't know how that happened), they were 18 and 23. It wasn't long before he proposed. He had a good job in a kosher butcher store. He had a trade. He could make a living.

The year was 1928. They were married January 6, 1929, just months before the stock market crashed and the Great Depression changed everything.

Sam, my father, fell hopelessly in love with my mother and stayed in love all his life. He was not a tall man, and though no one in either family could be described as tall, my father was the shortest. He was perhaps five feet, not an inch taller. He had finely chiseled features, high cheekbones and almond-shaped dark eyes that always made me believe the family was descended from the Kingdom of the Khazars.

The Khazars were a tribe of Turks who may have originated in Mongolia. In the Middle Ages, they lived side by side with the Jews of Hungary and the Ukraine, between the Caspian and Black Seas. From 650 to 1016, they were a world power. Some historians credit them with stopping Mohammed's sweep across Europe. In the ninth century, the king of Khazaria and his nobles converted to Judaism, and their people soon followed. Though only the men in the Kingdom of the Khazars are believed to have converted, their women, too, lived Jewish lives. Since they were all Jews, the Ashkenazi Jews and the Khazars married into each other's families for the next thousand years. Most scholars agree that Eastern European Jews have genetic ties to the Jews of ancient Israel, Germany, where the language of Yiddish developed during the Middle Ages, and the Khazars.

The high cheekbones and almond shaped eyes were not the only physical features Eastern European Jews may have inherited from the Khazars. Red hair is another, and in every generation, there are redheads among the descendants of Itzak and Esther. It is likely that both families, through the centuries, married and had children with Jews whose lineage could be traced to the Khazars.

Like many small boned men, my father was wiry and strong, and it was easy for him to pick up a side of beef and carry it into the huge refrigerator in the kosher butcher store.

Florence, my mother, was an inch or two taller than my father. In her youth, she was built like a twig, slim and flat chested. Her older brother and best friend, Lou, teased her mercilessly, and when Sam came courting, Lou asked Sam, "Are you sure you want to marry my sister? She looks like a boy."

She weighed 98 pounds when she married. The engagement and wedding portraits show a slim, pretty girl, her dark hair pulled back in the style of the 1920's. There is another photo, taken just a few years later, that shows her fine young features lost in fat. She was a nursing mother. She was never thin again. But she was not expected to be.

Florence and Sam in their engagement photo, 1928.

Florence, the Beautiful Bride, 1929.

The Old Customs Die Slowly

My bubbe, Malka, used all of her considerable power to keep my parents' wedding from taking place. It was not that my father was an unsuitable son in law. It was that there was an older daughter, Ida, who was not married.

She told Sam and Florence they could not marry before Ida.

It was a custom among Jewish families that probably came from the biblical story of Rachel and Leah. The older daughter must marry before the younger one. In the story of Rachel and Leah, in Genesis, Chapter 27, Jacob fell in love with Laban's younger daughter, Rachel. He asked Laban for his younger daughter in marriage. Laban wanted to marry off his older daughter, Leah, first, and suggested that Jacob marry Leah. He refused. But at the wedding of Rachel and Jacob, Laban tricked Jacob and substituted the older sister, Leah, as the bride. Jacob had to work for Laban seven more years before he could take Rachel as his second wife.

In addition to the biblical story, there were practical reasons for the older daughter to marry first. When the younger sister marries and the older is still without a partner, the older sister may be considered undesirable. In the life the family had recently left, it was common for parents to arrange the marriages of their children. And they made matches for their daughters by birth order.

Now, in America, my mother and father were in love and wanted to marry.

My Aunt Ida was four years older than my mother, earning money, buying fashionable clothes, going to concerts and theaters and falling in and out of love. She didn't feel like an old maid at 23. She stood up to her mother, and said, "You will not keep Fayga and Sam from getting married. I'll get married when I am ready. We are in America, not in Sobolifka."

My grandmother had to relent. One of Ida's granddaughters today wears the cameo pin Florence gave Ida at the wedding, in gratitude. Ida not only passed down the cameo. She also passed down the story. Her grandchildren know that she fought her mother for her younger sister's right to marry before her.

Not too many months after my parents' wedding, Ida met the man she would marry, Ben. He was tall and handsome, an actor who had worked in the Yiddish theater. He claimed to have acted with Paul Muni, who, by then, was a famous Hollywood star. When they met, Ben's acting days were over. He worked in a clothing factory.

Though my grandmother fought to keep her younger daughter from marrying before her older daughter, that battle was nothing compared to her campaign to keep Ida from marrying Ben. My Uncle Benjamin Berkowitz was a widower with two young sons in an orphanage, and a little girl cared for by his late wife's parents in Atlantic City.

The American Jewish community provided a network of services during the years of immigration. Among them were institutions for orphaned children. In every city with an immigrant Jewish population, there were "Homes" like the one in Philadelphia. Mothers died in childbirth and from tuberculosis. Fathers worked long hours and couldn't afford child care. Jewish Foster Homes (they were never officially called orphanages) filled the gap.

Malka chose to ignore the history of her own sister, Yetta, who had married Moishe and mothered his three children. To my bubbe, the difference between Yetta and her daughter was that Yetta had been divorced in the *shtetl*, making her a woman with a history. A damaged woman, no longer a virgin. Her opportunities for marriage were limited to older men and widowers, like Uncle Moishe, who had children to raise. Her daughter, Ida, had no history. And my bubbe didn't like Ben.

The conflict between Malka and Ida dated back to Ida's childhood, and Malka had less power with Ida than she had with her other children. Ida and Ben married in the same year as my parents, 1929. There was no honeymoon. Instead, they went straight to Atlantic City to take Ben's daughter home. Perhaps he had not been a devoted father. Perhaps he had not made regular visits to his motherless child. The grandparents closed the door in his face when he came to them with his new wife. They refused to give the child up.

He and Ida didn't persist. They were starting a life together with two half grown boys. Both sisters, Florence and Ida, had hard times ahead of them.

Hard Times in America

To immigrant young Jews struggling to earn enough money to pay rent and feed themselves, the stock market crash in 1929 may have been something other people worried about, real Americans with property and investments and money in the bank.

But the Depression kept ordinary workers and storekeepers a step away from poverty for a dozen years. They were marked by it forever. For the rest of her life, my mother never opened a charge account, never bought anything on credit. If she borrowed a quarter from a friend, or was a dollar short at the grocery store, she retraced her steps and paid her debt within an hour.

A year and a day after their wedding, January 7, 1930, my mother gave birth to her first child, a baby girl, whom my parents named Gilda. She was the second of Malka and Goddel's grandchildren to carry Goddel's name.

There was something wrong, though. So many years later, and all I know is that there was something wrong. Gilda was a sick baby. She didn't sleep. She didn't eat. She didn't sit up or turn over. She cried all the time. There is one photo of Gilda in my mother's photo album. It shows a stiff infant, a grim look on her face, no hint of a smile, the eyes without expression. Across the baby blanket on which Gilda is lying, in my mother's handwriting, are the following words: Gilda Litz, born, January 7, 1930. Died, October 19, 1930.

Cousin Fencie, the other Florence in the family, who was Yetta and Moishe's daughter, remembered the baby.

"I was 12 or 13 when your mother had your sister," she told me. "I used to go to her apartment after school. Sometimes, I slept over on weekends. My mother sent me there. 'Go help Fayga,' she would tell me. 'She needs help with the baby.'"

After Gilda died, my mother stopped lighting candles on Friday night. Even when I was growing up, though every Friday she cooked and baked and served a traditional Shabbat dinner, she did not light candles.

"I would not light candles to honor a God who let a child suffer so much," she once told me.

She always lit the candles on Jewish holidays. She recited *kaddish* on the anniversary of her father's death, and on the other days of the year that she was obligated to. And later, when she was a grandmother, she returned to lighting the Friday night candles.

Finding My Sister

Every year of my childhood, before the High Holidays, Rosh Hashanah and Yom Kipper, we went for a long drive to the cemetery to visit the dead. Going to the cemetery before the High Holidays was not a sad day. It was a day of driving in a caravan of cars filled with uncles and aunts and distant and close cousins whose families were all members of the Heisiner Independent Young Men's Society. The *verein* had purchased a large piece of ground in the old section of the cemetery in the early years of the members' American lives, when their members were, indeed, "young men." A generation later, when all the graves in that section were filled, the *verein* bought another piece of ground in the new section of the same cemetery.

The new section was where we went before the High Holidays. There, prayers for the dead were recited for our two cousins, Paul and Marvin Litz, who died at 18 and 19 during World War Two, and for the great aunts and uncles who had lived such long lives that there was no room for them in the old *verein* section.

My parents could have slipped away and taken a walk to the old section to say a prayer at their first child's grave, but they never did.

At least, not in my memory.

Now, I go to the cemetery by myself. The Heisiner Independent Young Men's Society is no more, and if it were, my generation would not be members. Still, I go to the cemetery before the High Holidays and talk to my mother and father and leave a stone on their graves.

On my last visit, I left my car at the circle in front of my parents' graves and took a walk to the old section to look for my sister's grave. I had no intention of doing so when I stood at my parents' graves. It was a sudden impulse. To find Gilda. To connect with what might have been.

I wasn't even sure where the old section was. Soon, I found a narrow, shabby walkway, too narrow and too broken up for cars. I turned into it.

I walked and walked up that broken path. On the left and the right, mixed in with the larger monuments, were hundreds of small gravestones marked with children's names and their dates of birth and death. Children who, like my sister, had died in infancy. Others who had died of childhood illnesses, of tuberculosis or pneumonia. "Our beloved daughter," said the tombstones. "Our precious son." Names in Hebrew and English.

Still, I had not found Gilda's grave. I grew tired and frustrated. It was a forest of death and what was I doing here? I would go home, I decided.

At that moment, I tripped over a broken piece of granite, a huge piece with ragged edges as sharp as my father's butcher knives. I could feel the granite cutting through my Indian summer shirt and jeans, bruising my back, my legs. I lay still for a moment, resting on the cold stone, until I caught my breath and checked my wounds. Then I looked around me.

I had not fallen on an anonymous broken gravestone. I had fallen on the remains of a huge, once grand, now shabby and neglected entrance to the first burial grounds of the Heisiner *verein*. The broken columns to my left and right reminded me of Victorian cemetery art. A curved piece of granite, as time worn as the columns, joined them, setting the area apart from the rest of the cemetery. My grandfather Nathan's name was carved into the granite in English and Yiddish, and so was the information that he was the founding president of the Heisiner Benevolent Organization, the first *verein* organized by the men of Heisin.

I lay there, astonished. I looked again, and saw my grandfather's gravestone straight ahead of me, the only one inside this separate enclosure. Then, I turned my head to the left, just a few feet from my grandfather's grave, and there was my sister's small stone.

It was as if Nathan had directed me. *"Hinanie,"* he called, as I fell. "Here I am," and "Here we are. Your sister is with me."

The Great Depression and the American Generation

It was hard for Florence, barely 20 years old, to accept the death of her baby. My young father didn't know how to help her. So he went to see their family doctor, and followed the doctor's advice. "Get her pregnant again," he told my father.

My brother, Norman, always referred to as *"Norella mit the shaine blueva oigen,"* Norman with the beautiful blue eyes, was born on June 26, 1931, and was adored by everyone in the family immediately.

Though I was born 22 months later, and my baby photos show a reasonably appealing infant, there was never any question as to who was the star of the family. "You were an ugly baby," my mother told me, adding, "It wasn't that you were so ugly. It's just that compared to Norman, you were ugly."

In September, 1930, Ida gave birth to her first child, Pearl, a blond, curly haired little girl who looked like a *shiksa*, not a Jewish child, but a child of Nordic or English stock. Her father, Uncle Ben, doted on her.

By now, my parents, Florence and Sam, had rented a storefront with "living quarters" in South Philadelphia. My mother stood side by side with my father all day cutting chickens, slicing beef, and tending to the store. Conveniently, they lived a city block away from the hospital where I was born. She went into labor hours before the first seder, Passover, 1933. My father was busy filling the Passover orders. The store was full of Jewish women buying for the holiday. When she told him it was time to go to the hospital, he got angry. "My wife," he said, "Just before the holiday, she chooses to go into labor! I can't leave the store."

She walked to the hospital alone, signed herself in, and gave birth to me.

There was a photo of me in a playpen, in front of the store, alone. She told me she always left me in the playpen and went back to the store to wait on customers.

When my brother was four and I was two, they moved again. This time, with a loan from the Heisiner Independent Young Men's Society, they were able to buy a store with a "dwelling" in a neighborhood called Feltonville, in the northeast section of Philadelphia. Feltonville was one of Philadelphia's many neighborhoods that are almost small towns. We lived in a village in the middle of a city. The year was 1935, still a hard time for anyone to make a living. Our store was on a wide street, Wyoming Avenue. There were trolley tracks on Wyoming Avenue, and busy lanes filled with cars and trolleys all day long.

On one corner of our street was a fruit store. Next to it was a grocer, and we, "Samuel Litz, Kosher Butcher," were third. On the other side of our store was a shoemaker, then a barber shop, and at the far corner, a gas station. My earliest memory is of my father carrying me, half asleep, from the number 75 trolley, late on a Friday or Saturday night. My mother walked behind us with my sleeping brother in her arms. We were coming home from visiting the family, in South Philadelphia or Strawberry Mansion.

My brother, Norman, and my cousin, Pearl, were six months apart. Often, we slept at each other's houses, or we fell asleep in whichever house we were in, so our parents could continue their visit. Pearl and Norman tormented me, throwing me out of our bed, making me sleep on the floor. I was an easy mark. Not only was I the youngest of the three of us, I was also chubby and clumsy. Nobody ever said I was the beauty of the family. Nobody ever noticed my almond shaped eyes, which were not brown,

I learned when I was in college (and boys began noticing me), but hazel, with specks of gold in them.

Norman became a neighborhood baseball star almost as soon as he was old enough to throw a ball. It was my responsibility, every night at dinner time, to walk to the neighborhood park and get him to come home. It was hard to pull him away from the baseball diamond.

Aunt Ida and Uncle Ben were getting through the Depression with the money they earned in their little cleaning and tailor shop, and Ida working the night shift at a cigar factory in walking distance of their store and living quarters.

All day long she cooked and cleaned, did the tailoring for the customers, mothered the young boys, Jack and Sol, and her own two children, Pearl and then Gilbert, born in 1937. Ida, the round and pretty blonde who had embraced the freedom and excitement of America, was now working like a mule, and the roundness of her younger years had turned to shapeless blubber. I remember once, as a child, seeing her naked. She had just come from the bath, and we were not a family reared on modesty and privacy. Aunt Ida's rolls covered her private parts. Every part of her body was too soft, too much. Years later, when she was diagnosed with diabetes, she measured everything she ate, followed the doctor's orders, and was once again a round and pretty woman — but never a healthy one.

Uncle Benny was her prince. He had his good points. He was handsome. He had a sense of humor. But my grandmother Malka never really made peace with Ida's choice of a husband.

As a little girl, I remember being at Aunt Ida's and Uncle Ben's home for our "summer vacation." In the days of the Depression, we didn't have money for a week at the nearby Jersey shore. None of us went to day camp. We played city games. The girls played hopscotch and jacks. The boys played baseball, or lay on the hot cement pavement playing games of marbles. On the most humid days of summer, we opened the fire hoses and cooled ourselves in the spray of cold water. My father had a bicycle that he used to deliver orders to his customers. My brother and I took turns riding it.

Every summer, Norman and I went to Aunt Ida's for a week's vacation, and Pearl came to our house for another week.

Though we were all poor, and our mothers worked hard, helping in the store, cooking and cleaning, Aunt Ida's life was different from my mother's. Ida, before she left for the night shift at the cigar factory, cut vegetables and put up huge pots of boiling water when she wasn't measuring a customer's hem length. Uncle Benny liked soup every day.

When I vacationed at Aunt Ida's house, I had to ask permission to call my mother on the phone. This was a time when we all signaled each other instead of wasting money on a phone call. You called your mother to tell her you had arrived at a friend's house by dialing your phone number and hanging up after the first ring. She knew you were safe and nobody had to pay the telephone company. But only at Uncle Benny's and Aunt Ida's house was there a lock on the telephone.

Malka's Sons and Their American Born Wives

In the first years of her daughters' marriages, Malka lived with her two sons in one or another of the rented houses in South Philadelphia. Her sisters, Inda and Yetta, were only a few blocks away. Her youngest sister, Frima, who had gone through revolution and pogroms in the *shtetl* with her, lived "behind the store" in an Irish neighborhood and later a Black neighborhood in North Philadelphia. Frima, her husband Abe, and their eldest son, Irv (whose name had been Israel in Europe), worked long hours in their store, while the two American born sons of Frima and Abe, Morris and Philip, did what American-born children of immigrants do. They went to school and helped in the store.

Nobody had automobiles. That didn't keep the family from seeing each other. They transferred from one trolley to another like the seasoned city residents they quickly became. The sisters and their husbands played cards together. Sometimes, the women stole away from their stores and met downtown, where they shopped in Wanamakers and Gimbels department stores and had lunch together in the Horn and Hardart restaurant.

My grandmother never stood behind the counter of a store. Her older son, Lou, kept his promise to his dying father. Though he must have had friends of his own— he was young and good looking —his life was tied up with the family, not only with his mother, but his sisters and brother and cousins. One of my earliest memories is of my Uncle Lou hoisting me on his shoulders, making me laugh. Whenever I found a quarter under my pillow on a morning, I knew Uncle Lou had visited while I was sleeping.

Sol, the disappointed young man who had to quit school to help the family, threw himself into the life of the man he wanted to be, an educated, upper class American man. As a teenager, my uncle developed a love affair with horses, and in his green and poor years, he began renting a horse on Sunday afternoons from a stable in the same Fairmount Park where his older sister, Ida, had discovered the concerts in the Robin Hood Dell during her first days in America. He became an accomplished horseman. It was a love affair that lasted all his life.

Years later, when he was no longer young and lean, he owned his own horse, and kept it in a stable in Fairmount Park. On Sunday afternoons, when he closed his grocery store, he rode his horse in the park.

He was not the only teenager who had to leave school during the Great Depression, nor was he the only one of his group of friends born in Europe. He and his friends had more spirit, more confidence in their futures, than their older brothers and sisters. They were the youngest immigrants, the most American. So, short of money though they were, they romanced the pretty American–born Jewish girls.

One Saturday night, Sol and his friends went to a party in Camden, New Jersey, just across the Delaware River from Philadelphia. There, my uncle met the girl he would marry. Her name was Doris. Her mother had died of cancer when she was 16. Her father remarried too soon. She was not happy living with a stepmother. They were very young. It was first love for both of them.

I imagine my handsome young uncle, the most American of Malka's children, who had excelled in his classes and spoke English as if he had been born in Philadelphia, not in Sobolifka, taking the ferry to Camden with a group of friends or walking across the Benjamin Franklin Bridge to court his American–born girlfriend who lived on the New Jersey side of the bridge.

Every Saturday night, he found a way to get to Camden to see Doris. He and his friends went to parties in the girls' homes, in living rooms behind the grocery stores and fruit stores in the Jewish neighborhoods of Camden. When the weather got warm, there were Sunday picnics in the open, grove—like parks east of Camden, on the road to Atlantic City. The big, aged trees provided shade from the hot sun and private spots where young lovers could hide.

Though Sol tried often to get his brother to come to the Camden parties, tempting Lou with descriptions of the pretty girls and the good times, Lou refused. He was four years older than Sol. He felt the weight of the whole family on his shoulders. Lou had no time for parties with young girls.

But one night when he must have been lonely, Lou went to Camden with his brother, and there he met Mildred. Mildred was 17. Lou was 22. Mildred, like Doris, was American born. She was the oldest of her parents' four children, and their only daughter.

Now, the brothers were both courting girls from Camden, girls who had grown up together.

The younger brother, Sol, married first.

Months before the marriage, Doris moved into Malka's house. It was a refuge from the stepmother she hated. Like many family stories, the story of Doris and my grandmother Malka has many facets. My grandmother once told me that she treated Doris as if she were "another child of my own." She came to her as a motherless child, eager for the maternal embrace Malka offered. Still, there were differences in the Yiddish speaking family Doris was joining, and the one she had come from.

Doris' mother had enriched her daughter's life by introducing her to the classical music both mother and daughter loved. Doris took piano lessons as a child, and practiced on the piano her mother had somehow found the money to buy. Her mother sat close to her while Doris played, encouraging her only daughter, glowing with pride at her child's talent.

The piano was a tangible tie between the mother who had died and her daughter.

When Doris moved into Malka's house, she brought her piano with her, according to Doris' eldest child, who says Doris came home one night to find her piano gone. Malka had sold it.

115

I can't imagine my grandmother selling a piano that belonged to a young woman who would soon be her daughter–in–law. My mother and her sister, Ida, often complained that Malka treated her daughters in law better than she treated her daughters. My grandmother knew that an unhappy daughter in law can loosen family threads. She once told me that a son would forget ten mothers for one night with the wife he loved. How she learned this folk wisdom is a mystery, since she came from a family of sisters, and a much younger brother. It may have passed down from each generation of mothers in law to the next.

Is it possible that the woman who sold Aunt Doris' piano was not Malka, but the wicked stepmother? Is it possible that Doris came to live with her husband's family before the marriage because her stepmother had sold her piano? There is no one left to ask.

Doris and Sol were married in March, 1935, and in April, 1936 their first child, Esther, was born. Some time between the day they married and the day their first child was born, my Uncle Sol became my Uncle Charles. Not only did he legally change his given name, he also changed his surname from Feinstein to Shoemaker.

He was a married man, soon to have a family to support. The Great Depression showed no signs of recovery. There were too few jobs open to him, or to the other young men in the cities and towns of America. In addition, it was a time when a Jewish name like Feinstein could keep a young man from getting a job. He needed a job, any job that would pay enough to support his wife and child.

My uncle, marked as a Jew as Sol Feinstein, could be any American as Charles Shoemaker. And there was another reason for his choice of the name "Shoemaker." He was honoring the father he did not remember. His father's name was Goddel Sapoznik, and Sapoznik is a

Russian word that means "shoemaker" or "boot maker." By choosing the surname, Shoemaker, my Uncle Charles was claiming the name the family had to discard when they came to America.

Whether his primary reason was to claim his father's name or to carry an "American" name, he was following in the footsteps of actors and writers and business leaders who had tossed off their ethnic names for the more American names they adopted.

In Philadelphia, there were two major commercial bakeries that hired young men as truck drivers. Every day, before dawn, these truck drivers went to the commercial bakery where the loaves of bread were baked and packaged, and filled their trucks with the fresh packages. Then, they spent the day driving from small grocer to small grocer, delivering loaves of bread to all the stores on their "route." The commercial bakeries paid their drivers good salaries for the work they did, but they didn't hire Jews. In the 1930's, and into the next decades, anti-Semitism was openly practiced in business and industry, as well as in universities, all over America. There were no anti—discrimination laws. Jews, as well as African Americans whose ancestors had come to America generations earlier as slaves, were turned away from many jobs.

Under his new name, he was hired by one of the two bakeries, and he remained a commercial bread truck driver through the Depression and into World War Two, when he and Doris opened their first grocery and butcher store. Soon, there was an ebony baby grand piano in the living room behind the store.

A month before their older daughter, Esther, turned 16, when their younger daughter, Sheela, was 10, Doris gave birth to their third child and only son, Jay. I remember the day we learned that Aunt Doris was pregnant a third time. We were at Bubbe's house, and the adults were seated at their usual spots around the dining room table. At 18, I was old enough to join them, but young enough to choose to be with my cousins. I heard laughter in the dining room. Teasing. Jokes with a sexual innuendo. My grandmother got up from her chair to bring more wine to the table, delighted with the news. Aunt Doris was giggling.

Unlike Charles and Doris, Lou and Mildred had a long and stormy courtship. It would be four years before they married. They didn't marry until she was 21 and he was almost 28.

He began bringing Mildred to the family early in the courtship. My mother, Florence, became Mildred's strongest ally. From the moment her brother brought his girlfriend to her home, my mother not only embraced her, but loved her. My grandmother found reasons to object, and one of them was that she and Lou's sweetheart shared the same name. Mildred's Jewish name was Malka. In Eastern European Jewish tradition, a child is named after a dead relative, to honor the loved one of a previous generation. In Eastern European Jewish superstition, another Malka might decree an early death for the older Malka. It was bad luck. Even though Lou was not so unsophisticated as to believe this, his mother's fears had an effect on him.

Mildred and Lou were married in September, 1936. In the formal family photograph, my grandmother is standing behind the bride and groom, her arms engulfing both of them, a wide, yet tentative smile on her face. My parents and aunts and uncles surround the bride and groom. On the front row, my brother and I are holding hands. Our cousin, Pearl, is seated across from us. She is dressed in a beautiful white dress as if she may have been the flower girl. Her long, blond hair is cascading over her shoulders. There is a pout on her face, probably because she wanted to sit with my brother and me, not at the other end of the row.

Mildred and Lou's wedding.

Mildred and Lou's honeymoon days ended quickly.

Lou had opened a new business, a sandwich shop on Vine Street, then the Skid Row of Philadelphia. There was a small apartment above the restaurant, and Mildred and Lou — and Malka — moved in.

Mildred and Lou were the restaurant operators, serving three meals a day and cups of strong coffee to the street alcoholics and other confused and homeless people who were their customers. It was not a romantic hideaway for Mildred and Lou. And from the first, there was a classic love triangle. Mildred was the other woman.

Was my grandmother, who believed that a son forgot ten mothers for one night with the wife he loved, an interfering mother in law? Did she say too much, and always at the wrong time? Was she winning the tug of war with the young bride for the young man's attention? And was the new husband, who, for so many years had been his mother's protector, torn between his two great loves? Probably.

One day, Lou came upon Mildred upstairs in their bedroom in the middle of the work day, her suitcase packed, getting ready to leave her husband.

She was crying as she tried to explain to him that she could not live this way, that they had no privacy, that Malka treated her like an outsider. He promised to talk to his mother. She cried more tears. She knew that she had lost the war. Lou's ties to his mother went back, in a straight line, to the promise he had made to his dying father when he was eight years old. She should have learned, in the years of their difficult courtship, that Malka would never share Lou with a wife.

He promised he would do better. He spoke softly. He told her how much he loved her. She put one stocking on. He pulled it off. He promised he would make his mother understand. She cried more tears and tried to put the stocking on again. He gently took the stocking off her other leg. The touch of love, the words of love, slowly broke through her armor. The stockings stayed off.

A few weeks later, Malka moved in with her youngest children, Charles and Doris. At least, that is what my cousin Esther remembers. Esther, who was an infant in Mildred and Lou's wedding photo, insists that Bubbe lived with her family. I remember visiting them in their little house in Strawberry Mansion, or perhaps it is the photographs taken through the years that I remember, photos of my grandmother holding the baby Esther, with her daughter in law, Doris by her side, on the steps of that house.

In my memory, throughout my childhood, my grandmother lived with us.

She was such a strong presence in our lives that we all believe she lived with us.

NINE — THE FAMILY THREADS ARE CUT

IN THOSE FIRST YEARS IN America, and Frayda's first years in Tashkent, the two branches of the family wrote occasional letters to each other. The old photograph of Frayda and her family that I remember from my childhood, the only evidence in my bubbe's house of the lost family, must have come in one of those letters from Tashkent, probably around 1928 judging from the ages of the two children in the photo. The letters, all in Yiddish, were not saved. Though I have never seen them, and there is no one left to tell me about them, I imagine that they shared little about the lives they were living.

How could it be any different? They were polarized. One was living in a new economic system, communism, dedicated to destroying the other's economic system, capitalism. There was a worldwide Depression.

The photo displayed in Malka's home: Frayda and David with their two children, Golya and Zena, in Tashkent, Uzbekistan.

Still, they tried to keep in touch. The family threads were stretched thin, but not broken. After a special occasion, like a wedding or the birth of a child, Malka would ask Yetta's husband, Moishe, or my father, Sam, to write a letter in Yiddish to her daughter in Russia. Often, she enclosed a few photos.

I can only imagine the pain my aunt felt when she opened an envelope and photographs of beautiful young women and handsome young men poured out. The brides were dressed in silks and satins, each holding an extravagant bouquet of flowers, everyone in the family in formal dress, as if they were, as a song of the times went, "as rich as Rockefeller."[7]

---

7   The song, "The Sunny Side of the Street," music by Jimmy McHugh, lyrics by Dorothy Field, was written in 1930.

At a family wedding,
Malka and her
handsome sons.

Pearl, Norman,
and Sissy at the
same wedding.

How could she have known that the voluminous wedding veils were rented from the fabric shops on Fourth Street in the immigrant neighborhood of South Philadelphia, that the elegant silk and satin dresses were borrowed, or rented, or sewn by a talented seamstress who lived a few doors away? Frayda must have thought her sisters and brothers were the capitalists her government blamed for all the world's ills.

By 1936, the year of Mildred and Lou's wedding, Stalin had tightened the noose around the people in the Soviet Union, whether they were in Moscow or the Ukraine or Tashkent.

One by one, all of Stalin's comrades who had led the revolution with him and were the thinkers and leaders of the new system were killed. There were show trials. Communist party leaders and intellectuals, including most of the Jewish writers, were tortured and forced to confess to crimes against the state, though they were innocent.

The terror extended to the masses, workers like my aunt and uncle who lived in one of the huge, concrete blocks of apartment buildings that the Communists built to house the people flocking to the Soviet Union's cities.

The walls were paper thin in those buildings. The mailboxes had no locks. There was little privacy. Everybody knew everything about their neighbors, but nobody knew who was a friend, and who was an enemy, an informer. Stalin's terror was an infection that spread from the Politburo to the arts to every corner of the Soviet Union, even Central Asia.

"Momma," said my aunt's 15 year old son, Golya, the child whose birth had kept her in the *shtetl*, "We must stop getting letters from America. Someone will report us."

She knew her son was right. She stopped writing.

And that is how the thin threads connecting the family were cut. It was the Soviet branch who broke the connection, to save themselves.

Ten — Our American Childhoods

Living Behind the Store

WE MOVED TO FELTONVILLE WHEN I was two years old and Norman was four. In our new neighborhood, there were other kosher butchers, but only a few, and they were blocks from each other. Our store was long and narrow. There was a butcher block near the front door, and another butcher block at the far end of the store. Connecting them was the counter and refrigerated display case, which was always filled with chickens and racks of beef and lamb, briskets, large slabs of bloody liver waiting to be sliced.

Before the Jewish holidays, when it was extra busy, my father brought live turkeys home and put them in our cellar. The cellar was dark, and smelled of coal, and was not exactly a healthy playroom. My brother and I spent hours in that cellar playing with the turkeys as if they were our pets, though we sadly had to accept the fact that they would soon be killed and eaten.

Every evening, my father scrubbed the day's remains from the two butcher blocks with a wooden brush that had sharp metal tips. In the early days, before he drove a car, the meat was delivered by Benny, the wholesale man. I remember him coming to the store almost every day. He was huge. All day long, he carried sides of beef on his muscled arms and shoulders into stores like ours. Later, when my father bought his first car, he woke when it was still dark and we were asleep, and went to the kosher slaughterhouse to buy the meat and fresh fowl he needed.

Separating the butcher shop from our living quarters was a small area that held the walk–in refrigerator where my father, small though he was, carried the sides of beef. All day, he half ran, half walked back and forth to move his stock from the huge, square, icy refrigerator, to find just the right piece of meat for each customer. In the same cubicle, a few inches away, there was a gas burner. That was where my mother and father singed the feathers from the chicken and other fowl each customer chose. I think we smelled of burnt chicken feathers all the time. I know our living quarters did.

There was a small parlor and kitchen behind the store and refrigerator/gas burner cubicle. My mother toiled mightily many nights washing the floors of the living area on her hands and knees, trying to win her battle with the smells and the sawdust and the remains of raw meat.

They often ate their meals standing up, at the kitchen sink, because from that vantage point they could see their customers enter the store. One of them would leave their lunch or dinner to wait on the customer.

One of my best childhood friends was a blonde, pretty little girl whose mother was Irish and whose father was Jewish. Another was a dark haired beauty named Maria, whose parents were from Albania. Her mother never spoke a word of English and wore her hair in an old woman's knot. Every Sunday, Maria and her older sisters, all as beautiful as she, went with their parents to the Albanian church, a half hour away on the trolley car.

The gas station and auto repair shop at the other end of our street took up the whole corner of Wyoming Avenue and Whitaker Avenue. The gas station was owned by a Jewish man, another Benny, who had a very Jewish surname. Benny had married a Catholic woman and converted to Catholicism. This was unheard of in our world. Benny and his wife and three daughters lived in a small bungalow on the grounds of the gas station, a few short steps from the gas tanks. Every Christmas morning of my childhood, my brother and I hurried to their house as soon as we had breakfast. There were toy trains running around the Christmas tree, a houseful of new toys and clothes, all kinds of sweet goodies.

Benny's three daughters went to Catholic school, not to the public school we attended. Even as a child, I wondered if their schoolmates were nice to them, if they fit in. The only cousins who visited were their Catholic cousins. My mother insisted Benny had once told her he kept a mezuzah in his pocket. (A mezuzah is a small parchment holding words from the Torah, usually fastened to a wall in a wood case, or placed inside a small pendant hanging from a chain to be worn as jewelry. Like the wall piece, the pendant with its scroll is a declaration of the Jewish faith.)

Despite Benny and his Catholic family, and Maria and her Albanian family, I need only look at my graduation picture from the Clara Barton Elementary School, which hangs on a wall in the basement of my home, to remember that I lived in a neighborhood that was overwhelmingly Jewish. The group photograph shows 106 eighth graders, each one of us in an inch square photo. In a class of 106, I count 76 whom I knew to be Jewish. The president, vice president, and secretary—treasurer of our class were Jewish.

The Irish and Italian children went to the Catholic school next to St. Ambrose Catholic Church with Benny's three girls. They lived on streets where Christmas trees and window wreaths decorated every house in December. We lived on streets where boys played marble games with acorn nuts on city pavements during the Passover week, and a small Chanukah menorah was lit in every house each night of Chanukah. My father gave us a shiny quarter when he lit the first Chanukah light, a nickel on the second night, and a penny every night until the week of Chanukah was over.

A few years after we moved to Feltonville, a whole new neighborhood of Philadelphia was built just a few miles northeast of us. Block after block of neat row houses sprung up. Though most of the development of that neighborhood was toward the end of World War Two, there were enough blocks of new houses built closer to our row of stores to benefit the produce store on the corner, the grocery store next to us, and our kosher butcher shop. My father got on his bicycle to deliver orders to his customers. In the summer, and sometimes after school, my brother, Norman, rode the family bicycle to the new houses a half mile away to deliver orders.

The Smells and Sounds of a Jewish Neighborhood

Thursday was the busiest day of the week in a kosher butcher store, as the Jewish women prepared for the Sabbath. The traditional Friday night dinner was chicken soup, roast chicken and briskets, noodle kugels, apple cake and cookies for dessert. Always, there was a fresh *challah*, the traditional twisted white bread, on the table, purchased at the bakery two blocks away on Wyoming

Avenue, or at Herman and Rose's grocery store, next door to our butcher shop. Everything else was lovingly prepared by our immigrant mothers, who measured themselves by the empty plates and overfed bellies of their children and husbands.

Getting ready for the Sabbath was simple compared to the frenetic preparation for the Jewish holidays. The Jewish housewives who were our customers were experts at choosing the best chickens and turkeys and briskets in the store, often making my father or mother go back and forth to the walk—in refrigerator until they were satisfied. Then, they boiled and baked and sliced and got their kitchens and their children ready to observe the coming holiday.

Somehow, my mother, Florence, found a day before each major holiday, Passover and Rosh Hashanah and Yom Kippur, to go to the old immigrant neighborhood of South Philadelphia with her mother, her sister, Ida, and sometimes, one of her sisters-in-law. They were all, except Bubbe, stealing time away from their stores.

They stopped for a quick visit with Yetta, still at the same living quarters behind the candy store that had been their haven when they came to America as new immigrants. Often, Yetta walked with them to the fresh fish store. There, frisky, fat carp and whitefish swam in water tanks, unaware that their last moments were near. The women, at least three deep, pointed to the fish they chose, and kept a watchful eye on the storekeeper as he killed, then skinned and deboned, cut and wrapped their purchase.

There were fish stores in our neighborhood, but the fish there were not swimming friskily. There were no live fish. And in the eyes of the Jewish housekeepers of my childhood, that made a difference in freshness.

Remember the Sabbath and Keep it Holy

Like every kosher butcher store, our store was closed before sundown on Friday, and remained closed till Saturday after dark. Every Saturday afternoon, my parents took a nap. They closed their bedroom door. After their nap, my father read the "Jewish Forwards" newspaper, out loud, to my mother. He read all the weekly chapters of the Isaac Bashevis Singer novels, first published as serial chapters in the Forwards. He read the "Bintel Brief," an advice column, heartbreaking letters from abandoned wives and unhappy husbands, workers complaining about their bosses. He read her the news from Europe, and it was not good news in the late 1930's and early 1940's—reports on Hitler's actions, the Stalin years, looming war clouds.

Saturday afternoon in bed was their gift to each other. It was part of a long Jewish tradition that on the Sabbath, it was a *mitzvah*, a blessing, to make love to your spouse.

It didn't take long for me to figure out what was going on during my parents' nap time.

Malka—Citizenship Class and Suitors

In the days of my childhood, my grandmother wasn't the only one in the family who spoke broken English. Yiddish was the native language of her sisters and their husbands, and the women who were their friends. Yiddish was the language they spoke when they were together. Though our parents' generation, those who were born in Europe, spoke English without a noticeable accent, they were more comfortable in Yiddish. My father, who came to the

131

United States as a 13 year old boy, counted in Yiddish. I remember him sitting at the kitchen table paying his bills. He did the arithmetic in a soft voice, always in Yiddish, never in English. Though my mother read the Philadelphia Daily News every day, and was addicted to romance magazines like "True Story" and "Modern Romance," her handwriting was childish. She was embarrassed at what she knew to be her terrible spelling skills. My father's newspaper was the Yiddish newspaper, "The Jewish Forwards."

My parents had neither the time nor the energy for "night school."

My grandmother had the time. Like many of her friends, the women in her "society" groups who had never had schooling in the old country, she became a student.

I couldn't have been more than six or seven when my bubbe enrolled in her first citizenship class offered at night at the Clara Barton Elementary School. Generations of immigrants learned to read and write in the English language at the citizenship classes offered through the public schools. For many, it was the first step toward further education. For others, it simply made them more comfortable in their new country.

Malka enrolled again and again in the citizenship class, and all she ever learned to write in English was her name. She never learned to read.

It was not because she was unable to learn. It was because of the way she saw herself, as the daughter of a respected man in the *shtetl*, Itzak *stolyar*, as the wife of an equally respected man, Goddel. She was the teacher, not the student.

I was a child in first or second grade. She was a student of the citizenship class. We were studying at the kitchen table together, I, doing my homework, she, trying to decipher the letters of the alphabet, to solve the puzzle of the English language. She beckoned me to her side of the table, as she proudly read a line of the page her teacher had assigned the class. Again, and again, we replayed the same scene.

"No, Bubbe," I corrected, with the confidence of a bright student who was never afraid to raise her hand in class.

After a few of my corrections, she stood up to her full height, which was not very tall, and admonished me, "You are teaching me? I am the grandmother. You are the child!" "*Ich bin da bubbe. Die bist da kind!*"

She silenced me quickly. I was being disrespectful.

She hid her illiteracy with confidence and inborn dignity. She was Itzak's daughter and Goddel's wife. She had lived at the top of the hill.

During the years Bubbe lived with us in Feltonville, there was always a man in her life. Her sons and daughters had all married. She was a grandmother of many children. Now, so many years after the short lived and disastrous marriage arranged by Uncle Moishe when she and her children were new to America, she was free to make a life of her own.

With her sisters and their husbands, she went to the Yiddish theater and to the *verein* social events. The women shopped at department store sales and sat at each other's kitchen tables, simply being sisters. And there were so many family events, holiday dinners and new babies, bar mitzvahs and weddings.

Suitors came and went. I remember one, especially. He was a tall, imposing man with a fringe of white hair around his bald head. In my memory, it seems that he was a part of her life for a long time. Every time he came to our house, he brought a box of candy for us, the grandchildren. Years later, I learned that he had left a wife and children in Europe. They were trapped there when World War Two broke out. Who knew if the Nazis had reached his village?

Believing that his wife and children were dead, he proposed to my grandmother. "And if she lives through this war, and comes to America, what will you say to her, that you've married another?" my grandmother asked him. Then he suggested that he take my grandmother away for a weekend, and when they returned, they would tell people they had married. "Never," she said.

Eventually, he stopped coming to our house, and that was the end of the boxes of candy.

On the Boardwalk in Atlantic City and My Grandmother's Boarding House

Even during the Depression, people who barely eked out a living found a few dollars for a weekend or a week in Atlantic City in the summer. Sometimes, my father drove us to "the shore," which is how everyone referred to Atlantic City, for a day at the beach. On the two hour drive from our house to the shore, we drove past open fields where tall corn and oversized and juicy Jersey tomatoes grew. We stopped at the nearby fruit stands and bought fresh—picked fruit and vegetables. For the whole 60 miles, as he drove through small towns and farmland, my father sang to us in Yiddish. Though I thought that the songs were songs of his childhood, most of them were songs of the Yiddish theater in America. They told nostalgic stories of Jewish life in the small towns of Eastern Europe, of love and marriage, sitting under apple trees, the traditional Jewish life they had left behind.

I knew the words to all the songs. I sang loudly with my father. Today, so many years later, I still know the words and the music of the Yiddish theater.

One summer, my grandmother rented a boarding house in Atlantic City for the summer season. Malka became the "businesswoman" she had avoided being all of her life.

There were many boarding houses in Atlantic City. They were usually just a few steps, or perhaps a short block, from the Atlantic Ocean and the boardwalk and beach.

Those oversized Victorian houses are gone now. Even the streets are gone, replaced by giant casinos extending from the boardwalk past the blocks that once held houses where people like my grandmother rented rooms to families who were grateful for a short respite from the steamy summer heat of the city.

Each boarding house had many bedrooms of varying sizes, bathrooms shared by strangers, and a huge kitchen. There was often a long porch filled with rocking chairs and wicker sofas. There was always an outside shower, where children and their parents washed the sand off their feet and their bodies before they entered the boarding house.

In the kitchen, women who were strangers to each other shared a stove and a refrigerator and filled a shelf in the kitchen cabinet with groceries. They gave each other space and time to cook for their families. Sometimes, there was more than one family eating at the kitchen table at the same time.

When Malka rented her boarding house that summer of my childhood, she had to fill the rooms with vacationers each week. She had signed a lease, with her signature, the only two words she could write in English. She had taken on a financial responsibility.

She hired help to clean the house. She swept the sand off the porch. She baked cookies and made chicken soup so that the house would smell savory and sweet. She filled bowls with hard candy and salt water taffy. She charmed the young couples who came to her boarding house with her light step, her spotless housedresses, and the smells of her kitchen.

All the branches of the family came to Malka's boarding house, some for an afternoon, others for a week. Her sisters' children who lived in Baltimore rented rooms for a week. When their Philadelphia cousins drove down for a weekend or a day to be with them, the cousins sat on the beach, sharing family stories and watching each other's children become friends.

I was four or five years old that summer. One weekend, Uncle Charles and Aunt Doris took me with them to Bubbe's boarding house. Running on the beach with other small children, I sliced the bottom of my foot when I stepped on a sharp piece of glass. Uncle Charles carried me on his back for a mile or more, my dripping blood marking our way in the sand. I remember that it was a long, long walk until we reached the first aid station, where a doctor stitched me up.

Though she probably made a profit that summer, Malka never took on another business endeavor. It was too much work. My father and mother continued to take us to the seashore on an occasional summer Sunday, but it wasn't until World War Two, and the prosperity that came with it, that we spent summers at the seashore.

ELEVEN — OUR SICK BROTHER AND WORLD WAR TWO MEMORIES

YEARS AGO, AS I BROWSED through some of my mother's old photo albums, I came upon a postcard dated October 5, 1938. In my Aunt Mildred's handwriting was written, "Dear Mother, we can't wait till you come home with our baby brother. We love you. Sissy and Norman."

My younger brother was born on October 5, 1938. I remember the day they came home from the hospital. It was a school day. I was five, and Norman was seven.

I was waiting outside when the taxi rounded the corner of Wyoming and Whitaker Avenues and parked in front of our store. My mother walked out of the taxi carrying our little brother. I ran to her, and took a peek at the baby, whose name was Herbert.

When she went into labor with me, she walked to the hospital because my father was busy in the store. Now, five years later, she was still on her own. He couldn't close the store to bring his wife and infant son home from the hospital. His customers might go to another butcher shop in the neighborhood.

My baby brother would change all of our lives.

He was about six weeks old when he was hospitalized with his first bout of pneumonia. My mother blamed her mother–in–law, who had visited on a cold autumn day, and, my mother insisted, picked up her newborn grandson before she warmed up. Always, it's the mother–in–law who gets the blame. Actually, at six weeks, his mother's antibodies should have protected the baby from disease. And my mother was nursing him, an additional protection.

Soon it became apparent that something was wrong, terribly wrong, with this child. I remember my mother and father in the bathroom with him, filling the tub with steamy, hot water, trying to help him breathe easier. It was not unusual for him to run temperatures of 107 and 108 degrees. He went into convulsions. He had pneumonia as often as other babies had runny noses. There were many middle of the night emergency trips to the hospital. My mother and father left us alone in the house, and, in the morning, instructed us, "If anyone asks how your baby brother is, tell them, 'fine.'" We knew he was in an oxygen tent struggling to breathe, and to live. We knew that our aunts and uncles had been called and that they left their children alone at home to sit in hospital corridors with Florence and Sam through the night, waiting to see if Herbie would live or die.

I didn't know why she said, "If anyone asks how your baby brother is, tell them 'fine.'" I suspect she worried that customers would stop coming into their store, fearing a contagious disease. And it was a time people whispered about sickness, as if it was something disgraceful.

Soon, the pediatrician was coming to our house regularly. He usually came at lunch time, and after he examined Herbie, or gave him a needle, he twirled me around the living room. My mother always had the radio on. She loved the swing music and love songs of the 1940's. The pediatrician took a moment to give me some attention, to teach me to dance. He must have known I had a crush on him. And he felt very comfortable with our family. He was in our house often enough.

Herbie grew up sick and slow. He started walking much later than most children. He was at least three when he began to talk. He was frail, and pale, and bone thin. Before he talked, he pointed to whatever he wanted, and my father marveled at how smart he was, that with a pointed little finger and an "eh," he could make himself understood and get us to give him the pretzel, the piece of bread, the toy he wanted.

I remember the feel of his hand in mine, when I, the big sister, took him for a walk. The soft, boneless, baby feel of his hand — when he was six or seven years old.

He started first grade in the same elementary school Norman and I were getting ready to graduate, the Clara Barton School in Feltonville. He didn't learn much. He was sick at home or in the hospital more than he was in school.

Because of Herbie's frail health, my mother gave herself permission to rent a summer place in Atlantic City during the last summers of World War Two. The salt air was good for her sick child, and she had a few extra dollars. The Depression had ended. The United States was in a war economy. Many of our neighbors, both mothers and fathers, worked in defense plants with young girls who should have been planning weddings and having their first babies. The young men, including six of my older cousins, were fighting in Europe and Africa.

Every factory building was now a defense plant, producing uniforms and weapons, screws and bolts, whatever was needed by the armed services. We never saw a new car during the war years. The automobile manufacturers built submarines and tanks, troop carriers, fighter planes. People worked overtime.

My father's customers brought "ration stamps" as well as money with them when they came to our store for meat and poultry during the war. Storekeepers like my father and my uncles pasted those stamps into booklets the government distributed. Without a full book of stamps, they couldn't buy the next week's supply of foodstuffs for their customers.

If there were shortages on the home front—and there were—there was also a free dollar or two.

Summers at the Seashore—
and the End of the War

We spent the summers of 1944 and 1945, the last two summers of World War Two, in Atlantic City.

Every Wednesday afternoon during those summers at the seashore, my mother took a bus to Philadelphia, then two trolley cars to our store and living quarters. Thursday and Friday were the busiest days in a kosher butcher shop. My father needed her help in the store. They worked together behind the counter, my mother as adept at cutting a chicken into pieces as my father. After they closed the store, before sundown on Friday, they drove to Atlantic City in his car. Like commuting fathers still do in the short weeks of summer, my father drove back to his butcher shop on Sunday night.

Norman, my baseball star brother, followed our father's schedule. He stayed home during the week to deliver orders on the bike that belonged to all of us, when he wasn't pitching and winning baseball games.

I was alone with my brother, Herbie, when my mother was in Philadelphia. But I wasn't alone. There was always an aunt overseeing the children whose mothers, like mine, hurried back to the city and the store.

My job was to take care of Herbie. Every day, as I sat with my summer friends and my cousins on the beach, Herbie sat close to me. I covered him when a wind grew strong, held his hand when he walked into the ocean water. Every evening, I pushed him in his stroller on the boardwalk. He was a quiet little boy, more like a toddler than a child ready for kindergarten. But a too quiet toddler. A toddler who never got into mischief.

I pushed that stroller past all the grand hotels on the boardwalk. During the war, the hotels were military hospitals where soldiers recuperated from their wounds as they gazed at the soothing, peaceful Atlantic Ocean. The young men—they were boys, really—had blankets covering their mangled or missing limbs, even on a hot and sunny afternoon. I wasn't the only one walking on the boardwalk, or pushing a stroller. All of us, the children and their parents, the pretty girls and the old grandmothers, waved to the wounded young men.

I met my first boyfriend on the boardwalk. I was 11 and he was 12. I was taking my early evening walk with Herbie, and I walked into the penny arcade on the boardwalk. Jerry, a Jewish boy from another neighborhood of Philadelphia, sort of picked me up. Every day after that, I met him at the penny arcade on the boardwalk, using my little brother in his stroller as my reason to be there. The summer ended. I never saw him again.

The war came home to us between the summers of 1944 and 1945. Two of my young cousins died in the service of their country. They were the sons of the two uncles named Joe in my father's family.

The phone rang one late winter night, waking us up in our beds. Our parents dressed quickly and left the house. They didn't tell us where they were going or what had happened. When they came home, we learned that our cousin, Paul Litz, was dead, his plane shot down. He was barely 18 years old. Paul was a quiet boy who spent too many years in the Hebrew Foster Home for Orphaned Children after his mother died. The last time I saw him, we were at the house he lived in with his father and his second mother and their blended family. The younger cousins, and I was one of them, were sprawled on the living room floor, listening to "The Lone Ranger" on the radio. He walked down the stairs. He was in uniform. None of us raised our heads or got off the floor to greet him. "The Lone Ranger" was more important to us at that moment.

Our Great Uncle Joe and his wife, Aunt Fanny, lost their oldest child, Marvin Litz, when the military plane he was training in exploded in the sky in Arizona, killing all the young men on it. He was 19. His mother, Aunt Fanny, went into a depression when her child was killed. Great Uncle Joe, a gentle, sweet man, could not console her. Neither could her two younger children. In a time when there was no grief therapy, mourning families worked through their devastating losses one way or another. Uncle Joe rented a boarding house in Atlantic City, not unlike the one my grandmother had rented a few summers earlier. It was not because he wanted the business venture. It was because he thought the responsibility would be good for his wife. It would keep her busy.

The family rushed to rent rooms in Aunt Fanny's boarding house. Everyone wanted to help. That summer, I made friends with cousins I didn't know I had, and children who weren't my cousins, but were cousins of other cousins. When our mothers went back to the city to help their husbands in their stores, there were other mothers, related to us or not, who never hesitated to admonish us or feed us.

Aunt Fanny's boarding house was a beautiful, big house just a few steps from the boardwalk on one of the streets near the inlet. It had many bedrooms and bathrooms, back steps and side steps. The porch was huge, and there was another porch on the second floor, where the women who stayed all week played mahjong while their children slept and their husbands were back in the city working.

It was the summer of 1945, the summer the war ended. President Franklin Delano Roosevelt, the only president I knew in my 12 years, had died suddenly a few months earlier, on April 12. Now, we had a new president, Harry Truman. On April 30, Adolph Hitler committed suicide in his hidden bunker because he knew the Allies had defeated him and he would be tried as a war criminal. On May 8, the long war in Europe was over. The Germans surrendered. But the Japanese, their partners, held on.

All summer long, as the terrible photographs of the Nazi concentration camps were released, we learned of the murder of six million Jews, as well as gypsies, homosexuals, and the mentally ill.

On August 6, 1945, American planes dropped the first atomic bomb on Hiroshima, and three days later, August 9, they flew over the city of Nagasaki and dropped another atomic bomb. Thousands died in both cities. Thousands more were horribly burned, and would suffer the effects of radiation damage for the rest of their lives. Even the next generations would suffer. Radiation damage was responsible for many birth defects in Japan for generations.

In Atlantic City, our older cousins walked around with portable radios at their ears, waiting to hear that World War Two was over. Our mothers, too, listened to the news all day long. Everywhere, at the ice cream stands, the grocery store, as you walked past someone on the boardwalk, or sat near a stranger on a blanket at the beach, you listened to the radio.

On Tuesday, August 14, the Japanese emperor surrendered. Though the official date of the end of the war is August 15, 1945, when President Truman accepted the emperor's surrender, the celebrations began on Tuesday. It was wild on the boardwalk.

In Aunt Fanny's boarding house, the women baked and cooked in preparation for a victory party. Their men closed their stores and left their jobs to come to the seashore in the middle of the week to celebrate with their families.

Our mothers and the older children found aluminum folding tables and set them up end to end on the long porch. They had been stored away somewhere in the house, left by a previous landlady or the owner of the house. The women baked *kugels* and *knishes*, cookies and cakes. They chopped vegetables and made the salads of a summer picnic — potato salad and tuna salad, cole slaw and chopped chicken livers, and filled platters with the kosher cold cuts they bought from the local delicatessen. There were huge watermelons cut into slices, full bowls of fruit, fresh corn on the cob, the bounty of the season.

Bottles of schnapps emptied quickly as our parents and aunts and uncles toasted the end of the war. And there were tears. For all the young lives cut short. For the murder of Europe's Jews.

Twelve — The Russian Family— Did the Nazis Kill Them?

In the days and months after the war ended, we learned more about the horrors and torture endured by the Jews of Europe. We went to the movie theater to see a musical comedy, and a 20 minute newsreel preceded it. Film after film of emaciated survivors and piles of the dead flashed across the screen. The narrator, speaking in the background in his deep, sonorous voice, gave us the numbers, the details, but it was the photographs we would remember all our lives. Scarecrow–thin boys and men with eyes like holes in a piece of wood. The maimed children, their bodies deformed by Nazi medical experiments. Soldiers, Russian or American, liberating a camp, and the walking dead dancing with them. The number killed by the Nazis, six million Jews, was a statistic, not a reality. The photographs gave us nightmares.

We learned that in the Ukraine, there were no more Jews. The Nazi killing squads, the Einsatzgruppen, swept across the towns and villages where Jews had lived for centuries, lined up their victims, and shot them dead, a million and a half Jewish men, women and children.

There had been whispers before the war ended. The Jewish Forwards, as well as the New York Times and our newspapers in Philadelphia, printed stories told by the rare survivors who had somehow found their way to America during the years of World War Two, or smuggled a news report out. There was a Jewish girl in my class at school who spoke with a German accent. Her mother had a tiny store a block from our store, where she sold underwear and socks. There was no father. The daughter was very bright. She kept to herself. We didn't ask questions.

There were whispers, and even evidence, but who could believe that a slaughter like this could happen, in any war, in the middle of the 20th century?

When the first photographs of the Nazi death camps were released, my family must have believed that their sister Frayda and her family had met such an end. I think they had forgotten, or never really knew, how far Tashkent was from the Ukraine or that there was any town that had not been a killing field.

Indeed, the Nazis had murdered all the Jews of Sobolifka. Frayda would tell us of the slaughter of the people in the *shtetl* when she came to us so many years later.

THIRTEEN — MOON OVER MIAMI

Leaving Her Sick Child

IN THE FALL OF 1945, soon after the end of the war, my mother took her sick child to Miami, Florida, on the Silver Meteor train. She left her husband and her two older children and her duties in the store because the pediatrician who came to our house every week prescribed a warm climate for her sick son.

She spent a few days at a hotel in Miami Beach with Herbie, visiting the boarding schools that she had somehow learned about. My immigrant, unschooled mother would leave her youngest child, her sick baby, in the hands of strangers at a boarding school in Florida, as if she were a wealthy society parent who wanted to be free of her child.

Before she left him there, she went to a photographer in Miami Beach and had formal photos taken with her son. There are several of her and Herbie with the palm trees and blue skies of Miami Beach behind them. She is trying to smile. In the photographer's studio, the photographer seated Herbie at a round table, surrounded by a backdrop of mirrored walls. In every photo, there are repeated images of Herbie. In one, his hand is on his chin. In another, he is looking straight ahead. He is unsmiling, solemn. Neither happy nor sad.

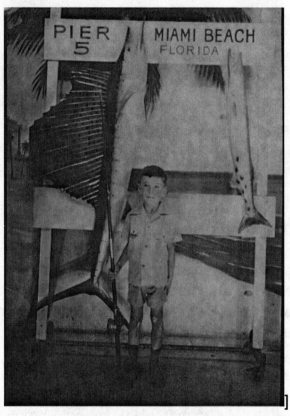

Herbie, alone in Florida.

I think my mother was sure he would die without her. I think she had the professional photographs taken because she didn't expect to see her child again.

She chose a boarding school. Herbie would be there through the winter. If the tropical climate of South Florida would save their child, if he was healthy all winter, she would leave her mother and her sister and brothers, and her husband would leave his family, and we would move to Miami.

I don't know how she left my brother there. She, who told the stories of his every illness with the dramatic effect of a Broadway actress, never talked about the farewell moments.

She started smoking that winter, and soon was smoking three packs of cigarettes a day and coughing constantly. She never broke the habit, not until the heart attack that killed her.

Every Friday, around lunch time, someone from the boarding school called to give my parents a report. He was a quiet, well-mannered child. He seemed to be adapting to the school. No, he did not cry for his family. And, most importantly, he had no fevers, no convulsions, no emergency trips to the hospital.

After my mother got the official report from the staff member, she spoke to Herbie. He cried pitifully. He asked my mother when he was coming home.

It was a hard winter for us all. Yet, I also remember it as a special time for Norman and me. We were both entering our teens. And since we were only 22 months apart, we shared the same friends. We were free that winter, free to bring our friends into the small living room behind the store, to have our first parties in the house, to be normal adolescents. I remember feeling guilty about how much fun I was having. The pall of constant sickness had left our family.

Another Separation of the Family

In April, I came home from school one day and Herbie was sitting in his seat at the kitchen table. Florence must have taken the train south to bring him home, but I have no recollection of being without her. She may even have spent a few days looking for a place for us to live in Florida, because she and my father had made the decision to sell the store and "dwelling" on Wyoming Avenue, and to move us all to Miami. Herbie had been well the whole winter.

I went to school in the morning, and when I came home at lunch time, he was there. He was quiet. It was as if he was a visitor in our house. It would take him awhile to return in his mind to the family. I remember that my mother asked him if he would like more milk. "Yes, ma'am," he responded. After he had said "yes, ma'am" three or four times to her continuing questions, she exploded, "Don't call me 'ma'am,' I'm your mother!"

He never stopped saying "yes, ma'am." He had learned the manners of a Southern boarding school, and the responses that were expected in that society had somehow worked their way into his brain.

My mother learned about a new development of small homes in Miami, and she knew three families from Philadelphia who were buying in the development.

The young men who had fought in World War Two were coming home and marrying the girls who had waited for them. All over the country, in Florida as well as Pennsylvania, there was a building boom. Whole communities, the first Levittowns, sprung up overnight.

Ours was not a Levittown, but it was a collection of neat, new houses, each filled with young families, and schools nearby.

She talked my father into buying the house, though he hadn't seen it. Years later, when she died, I told him, "Daddy, Mom told me you were a good husband." He responded, "I always did what she wanted."

Between April and September of 1946, we got ready to say goodbye to Philadelphia, to the extended family of aunts and uncles and cousins, to the neighborhood that was more like a small town than a city neighborhood.

I had just turned 13, and Norman was 15.

I remember a huge farewell party in somebody's house, but I have no memory of where it was. Every relative was there, the great aunts and uncles on both sides of the family and their children who were my parents' first cousins. They brought gifts for my parents, as if they were a bride and groom starting their life together. Mema Yetta's gift was a large, silky damask banquet cloth, which my mother kept folded as new. There was never an occasion important enough for her to put such a tablecloth on her dinner table. When she died, the folds had turned to permanent yellow lines. I threw the tablecloth out.

Everyone was trying to make this step a new beginning, not a sad parting of the family. Though it was nothing like crossing the Atlantic Ocean, leaving behind a sister, it was the same ripping apart of family ties. Long distance phone calls were expensive, and so were airline flights.

The day came when my father and my brother, with a packed car of our household belongings, set off on the three day road trip to Miami.

A day or two later, Florence, Herbie and I boarded the train. This time, only my two grandmothers and a few aunts were there to see us off. The men in the family were tending their stores. The farewells were noisy and dramatic, my mother sobbing, both my grandmothers wailing. It was as if they were reliving their last moments in the *shtetl*, as if they did not believe they would see each other again.

I, following Florence's lead, was out of control. As the train left Philadelphia's 30th Street Station, the crescendo from the platform increased dramatically, and my mother's sobs mirrored those of the family. We continued our loud crying for the first four hours of our train trip. Herbie, on the other hand, was impassive, unmoved.

The train was full of young men in uniform coming home after years fighting in Europe or Africa, and months in military hospitals like the ones on the Atlantic City boardwalk. Some had only one leg. Some had eye patches. Others were maimed in ways we could not see, though I was mature enough at 13 to understand that they were scarred, both physically and emotionally, from their war experiences. I remember that they looked at us with pity and curiosity, wondering what terrible calamity had befallen our family.

Eventually, we calmed down. My mother found the sandwiches and fruit she had packed. We ate. We slept. And when we awoke in the morning, a new world awaited me. Through the train windows, I saw the bright blue sky of Florida, clouds like cotton candy. In town after town, as the train swept through, there were miles of yellow and pink and pale green houses with white shingled roofs, so unlike the storefronts and cellar doors and pavements we had left. I stood at the landing between the cars of the train for hours, captivated by the beauty of my new home.

I have no memory of arriving in Miami and getting off the train, but I remember every moment of that train ride, as the sorrow of leaving turned to the excitement of a new life, and the shadow of sickness and the drabness of the old city was transformed to light and color and hope.

Amazingly, we were moving into a house not unlike the ones I had fallen in love with on the train. But our house wasn't finished.

Once again, family came to our rescue. My bubbe's Baltimore sisters had children living in Miami. I had never met the two great aunts who lived in Baltimore, and both were dead by the time we moved to Miami. But the family was connected enough so that my mother could call her cousin, Dorothy, to ask her to take us in for a week or two. Dorothy was a new bride. She and her husband, Sam, lived in a one bedroom apartment with a screened in porch. Norman and I slept on the porch, my parents in the living room with our little brother. We were there for more than a week or two.

In Miami, as in Philadelphia, we, the descendants of Itzak *stolyar* and Esther, of the *shtetl* of Sobolifka, were never without family.

Fourteen — Enemies, Once a Family

During the post World War Two years, our early years in Miami, our lost aunt was in Siberia with her husband.

David, a quiet tailor from the *shtetl* who worked in a clothing factory in Tashkent, earned a few extra dollars doing small tailoring from his home after hours. He made a hem for a worker whose only trousers, handed down from others in his family, were too long, or needed patching. A warm jacket many sizes too big for a small child would fit after David's skilled alterations. He looked at a torn and patched dress a woman brought to him and made a seam here, a pleat there, and the woman had a dress to wear. His customers gratefully paid him for his work. This was a criminal act in the Soviet Union. He was engaged in a capitalistic enterprise.

"Someone reported him," my cousin Zena, his daughter, told me years later, and he was sentenced to hard labor in Siberia. Frayda knew he would not survive without her. Though she was a trained and licensed midwife in Tashkent, she got permission from the authorities to follow her husband to Siberia. Or perhaps no permission was needed. Who would go to Siberia willingly, without being sentenced to do so, unless she wanted to keep a beloved husband alive through his hard prison term?

Frayda fed her husband hearty soups and hot bowls of *kasha*. She warmed his bed with the heat of her body. She wrapped wool scarves around his neck to protect him from the icy winds as he worked all the long hours of his imprisonment. Perhaps most critical to his survival, he was not alone through the years in the *gulag*.

But in Tashkent, her 19–year–old daughter, Zena, a medical student, was as lonely as if she was an orphaned five–year–old. She responded to the affection of a young student at the university, and by the time her parents returned to her, she had married and divorced, and had a baby girl to support.

"My mother should never have left me to go to Siberia with my father," she told me years later. "I was a child. I was lost without both of them."

The United States and the Soviet Union were enemies again. In Washington, the House Un–American Committee grilled writers and professors, Hollywood actors and Broadway stars, under oath, forcing them to admit that they had been members of the Communist Party in earlier years. Many of them had. Young intellectuals during the Depression, disillusioned by what they interpreted as the failure of capitalism, were drawn to Karl Marx's ideas. This was not a crime in the United States in the 1930's.

But now, with World War Two over, and Stalin tightening his grip around all of Eastern Europe, the Soviet Union was a threat to our treasured democratic way of life. Many of the young idealists who had flirted with communism were ruined. College professors lost their positions. Actors and writers were "blacklisted." They were on a list of talented people who could not find work, could not sell their novels and screenplays.

My immigrant parents and the aunts and uncles cringed when they read these news stories. And they were not interested in finding a sister who was a communist in communist Russia. Besides, she was probably dead.

They never talked about her. But the photograph in my grandmother's dining room, the photograph of Frayda and her husband and two small children, stayed where it was, reminding us of our lost family.

Then, in 1951, when Julius and Ethel Rosenberg, a young American Jewish couple who were communists, were arrested and found guilty of treason against the United States, every Jewish family in America was afraid, and ashamed—except, of course, the ones who were communists. The Rosenbergs were executed in 1953.

If our parents had not talked about their sister in Russia before, how could they talk about her now?

All that would change when the first letter came from Tashkent.

FIFTEEN — LIFE IN THE TROPICS

Our Sick Brother is Well

OUR HOUSE WAS A SMALL bungalow with a porch that held two or three chairs. There was a living room with a fireplace, a modern kitchen with electric appliances, and a dining room. Off the living room was a hallway that led to three bedrooms, one for my parents, one for my two brothers, and one for me. A screened–in back porch, called a Florida room, opened up to a quarter of an acre of greenery, our back yard. My father, the immigrant kosher butcher, planted banana trees and orange and lemon trees. My mother, the fatherless child from the *shtetl*, took pleasure in her hibiscus and crotons, which grew in abundance. The grass was thick under their feet.

My father rented space in a large food market in Miami Beach, in what is now the glamorous South Beach where the beautiful and famous people from all over the world come to be seen. Then, the neighborhood was filled with Jews, most of them in their retirement years, who, like my parents, spoke Yiddish fluently and kept their kitchens kosher. From the first day, my father was busy waiting on his customers. One evening, he came home and emptied his pockets and threw all the dollar bills and twenty dollar bills and fifty dollar bills on the living room floor in a flourish of excitement. It must have been before a Jewish holiday, perhaps Passover.

Herbie walked to the elementary school up the street from our new house. Norman and I were in 9th and 10th grade, getting used to the Southern accents of our teachers, trying to make friends. Most importantly, Herbie was not sick. He played outside with other children in the new development after school. He didn't get pneumonia. He wasn't hospitalized. My parents' sick child was well.

But my father was used to living behind the store. The 40 minute car drive from our little bungalow in Miami to his corner of the supermarket in Miami Beach made his day too long. When the one year lease in the big market in Miami Beach was near its end, he looked for a store closer to our home.

There was a new row of storefronts about two miles from our house, on a main street. My father investigated and found there were no kosher butcher shops nearby.

The Jewish Home for the Aged was across the street from the new row of stores. My father thought that was a sign that there were Jews in the neighborhood. Perhaps there were. But not many. And the ones who were there did not buy kosher meat.

Miami was a small, southern town in 1946. Miami Beach, a few miles east on the Atlantic Ocean, was the winter resort. In both communities, many of the transplants, like us, had resettled in Florida because someone in the family was sick. A father had a bad heart. A child had asthma, or allergies. In 1946, Herbie's pediatrician wasn't the only doctor who recommended a warm climate to his patients.

My little brother never really grew up, but we didn't notice that. We lived with him. Every year, he was promoted to the next grade in school. He didn't learn much. But none of the teachers in the school up the street ever called my parents for a conference. He was quiet. He never got into trouble.

Apparently, I was the only one who cared that he could barely read, that his math skills were as terrible as his table manners. Often, I sat at the kitchen table with Herbie, trying to help him with his homework. My mother stopped me. "Leave him alone," she said. "Whatever he'll learn, he'll learn. It's too much for him."

It was "too much for him" to prepare for a bar mitzvah, too. My traditional Jewish parents never took him to a synagogue or enrolled him in Hebrew School.

Herbie and his parents.

When he was old enough to know better, Herbie left the bathroom door wide open, even when there was a houseful of teenagers in the nearby living room. Once, when I was already in college, and my date and I were sitting on the sofa, I heard the stream of Herbie's urine as loud as if it was next to me. My date heard it, too. I was embarrassed. Later, when the two of us left the house, I confided to this bright young man that I worried that there was something wrong with my brother.

"Don't worry," he said. "I had a heart problem when I was a kid, and I was in bed a lot. My family babied me. I was very immature for a long time. He'll be all right."

But he wasn't.

The Poor Relatives

We had barely unpacked our things and settled into our new life when the visitors from "up north" came to visit. The old photo albums tell the story.

Here is a photo of Bubbe and Zayda and Yetta and Moishe, the sisters and their husbands smiling in their bathing suits in the Florida sun on a winter day. And here is a photo of Uncle Lou, who spent most of his visit building a shed next to the outdoor electric outlets. It became my mother's laundry room.

I can't imagine that Mildred and Lou closed their store to drive to Florida, or that Charles and Doris did the same. But they did. So did my father's brothers and their wives.

We got a letter from our two twenty something cousins in New York, the daughters of my grandmother's dead brother, Abe. Could they come to Miami on their vacation? Of course, my mother wrote back.

My cousin, Gloria, daughter of my father's youngest brother, Izzy, another kosher butcher, remembers spending a whole summer at our house in Miami with her younger brother. Her father was recuperating from a hernia operation. Her mother was running the store on her own, and my parents helped by taking the children for the summer.

I was not there that summer, or most other summers. I was up north, earning money in Philadelphia. Every summer after I turned 15, I stayed with Mildred and Lou in their "dwelling" behind the store and saved my earnings for college. I shared a room with their only child, Diane, who looked up to me as if I was her big sister.

In the late 1940's and early 1950's, salaries in Southern towns were notoriously low. Also, air conditioning was new, and not in everyone's home or office, or even in every hotel. Though South Florida had been a winter resort since the 1920's, and Miami Beach hotels drew vacationers who wanted to get away from the snow and cold during the winter months, it was not a great place to be in the hot, steamy summer.

One of Florence's favorite lines was, "I'll scrub floors so that you and your brother can go to college." I knew there was no money for my college tuition. Neither was there money for a few skirts, a pair of shoes, the things that young girls need.

My parents, who had worked as hard as their brothers and sisters, were almost penniless, despite the prosperity that came with World War Two and the years after it, the years we were in Miami. They were burdened with the medical expenses that kept their sick child alive.

When Herbie was born, in 1938, health insurance was in its pioneering years. Premiums were low because hospital costs were low. The medical breakthroughs during World War Two, and the development of penicillin, the first antibiotic, revolutionized medical treatment and provided doctors with many weapons. But costs spiraled. My parents told us that Blue Cross "threw them out" because of Herbie's constant hospitalizations. It is more likely that Blue Cross increased premiums to an impossible level, or sent them a form letter they didn't understand, indicating that they had used up all their coverage.

If the money was coming in during World War Two, it went out just as fast—to the doctors, the medicines, the hospitals that had kept our sick brother alive.

When my parents sold the store and "dwelling" in Philadelphia and bought the bungalow in Miami, they had little left. Worse, my parents owed thousands of dollars to their brothers and their wives. There was an actual number,

$10,000, a sum that was impossible to pay back, a sum that was equal to the cost of a house in the 1940's.

My father traded his kosher butcher counter in the Miami Beach supermarket—in a neighborhood filled with elderly Jews who kept their kitchens kosher—for a shiny new store across the street from the Jewish Home for the Aged in Miami. To do so, he borrowed money from the family in Philadelphia. I don't know why he went to the family instead of the Heisiner Independent Young Men's Society. My guess is that loans from the *verien* paid for the move, for the medical bills. There was a limit to the amount a shareholder borrowed. The *verein* was a financial institution, regulated by rules, and by law.

For the rest of their lives, my parents were in debt to those who were closest to us, their flesh and blood.

Florence walked around with torn stockings rolled down to sock length. She never spent a dime on herself. She tried to save a dollar or two from her house money, so that she could enclose $25 or $50 in the letters she wrote to the Philadelphia family.

Still, there was a representative of our family at every family bar mitzvah and wedding in Philadelphia during the years we were in Miami. My father flew to Philadelphia for the weddings and bar mitzvahs of his brothers' children. My mother took a plane or train to Philadelphia when her family celebrated a milestone. Sometimes, we missed the occasions that meant the most to us. My brother, Norman, stayed home with our father when our cousin, Pearl, married, though the two of them had been inseparable as children. Florence and I took the overnight train to Philadelphia. I was Pearl's maid of honor.

My mother learned about cheap, unscheduled airlines, the inexpensive way to fly. You never knew when the plane would leave. You were never sure the plane was in good shape. But the fare was affordable.

Once, when I took her to the airport to board an unscheduled plane for a family event, I sat in the waiting room for hours, watching Florence and the other passengers board, then a few minutes later, come down the ramp to the waiting room. Something was wrong with an engine. A half hour later, there was an announcement that the plane's passengers should board again. Then, they came down the ramp again. You had to have nerves of steel to take those unscheduled flights.

SIXTEEN — ALL THE YOUNG MEN ARE IN UNIFORM AGAIN

TOO SOON AFTER THE END of World War Two, we were at war again. Now, our enemy was North Korea, but the real enemy was the Soviet Union.

In June, 1950, Communist North Korean forces, assisted by the Chinese Communist government and funded and trained by the Soviet Union, invaded democratic South Korea. President Truman ordered ground forces and Air Force bombers to the area. In October, Chinese Communist troops crossed the Yalu River into Korea, and forced the mighty United States Marines into retreat that December at the Chosin Reservoir. Casualties were high. Enlistments were down. There were rumors and newspaper articles about a draft, one that would include college students.

At the University of Miami, where I was a student, and at other colleges, the young men were in a panic. In one fraternity house in Miami, half of the fraternity enlisted during one weekend. It was an epidemic of fear. Everyone knew that draftees went directly to Korea after basic training, to places like the Yalu River and the Chosin Reservoir.

My brother, Norman, walked into an Air Force recruiting center in Miami on a hot May afternoon. He told the recruiter he was a pitcher on the University of Miami baseball team, that he had a baseball scholarship. The recruiter responded that the Air Force needed him—to play baseball. My brother signed up for a four year enlistment.

Just a few mornings later, Norman, Florence, and I walked in a solitary, silent line, my brother leading, my mother and I following him, to the bus stop on South West Eighth Street, where the three of us would go together to the train station, and only two of us would return to our little bungalow on South West Fifth Street. My father was tending the butcher shop. Herbie was in school.

Though we had lived in our house four years, the street we walked on was unpaved, filled with the bleached stones and pebbles natural to Florida. To our left and to our right were tropical scrub trees and wild palm.

My mother walked a few paces behind my brother, stumbling here and there on a stone. I followed. The only sound from the three of us during that endless three—block walk was her stifled sniffle. She was trying to control herself, but Norman, in front of her, and I, behind her, knew her anguish. The bus arrived. The three of us boarded, took our seats. Still, not a word of conversation. The bus took us downtown, to Miami Avenue, to the Flagler East Coast Railroad Station. There, the three of us stood together waiting for the train that would take my brother away from us and out of his mother's protection.

The train came. My brother hugged us both, boarded quickly, and was gone in a moment.

Then, a flood erupted. "*Guttenu, Guttenu,*" she cried, first beseeching God, then bargaining with Him.

"Do not save the son who is already stricken," she wailed, every word in Yiddish, as if it were her only language. "If you have to take one of them, save the healthy one and take the sick one," she begged, or perhaps she ordered. "Take the sick one," she kept repeating. "Do not take the other one, the strong one." I tried to get her to stop her screaming, but soon I was as hysterical as she was.

Eventually, she calmed down. We went home.

A few weeks after Norman left, my college semester ended and I went north for the summer, as I did every summer, to stay with Aunt Mildred and Uncle Lou, to earn money at a summer job. At the end of every summer in Philadelphia, I came home with every dollar I had earned, and there wasn't a day that I felt as if I was taking advantage of my aunt and uncle's hospitality.

Only later, years later, would I learn from my mother that she had expected me to stay home that summer. She thought I knew how much she needed me the summer her son, "*Norela with the shaina blueve oigen*," Norman with the beautiful blue eyes, left.

She never asked me to remain in Miami, and if she had, I probably would have gone up north anyway. I was a young woman who wanted to live her own life. I dreamed of going to New York after I graduated from college, and, with my degree in journalism and clippings of the stories I'd written and the awards I'd won, I'd begin my career as a writer.

Love and Marriage

I stayed in Philadelphia longer than usual the summer of 1951. My best friend, Ellye, was getting married in late September in Newark, and I was her maid of honor. We had moved to Miami the same week, when I was 13 and she was 14. Our houses were around the corner from each other. By the time school started, we were inseparable.

When I returned to Miami after the wedding, I would enter my second year at the University of Miami on two scholarships. During my senior year in high school, the University of Miami set up a scholarship program designed to raise the academic level of its student body. The top students in each of the county's public schools were offered full, four year scholarships, and I was one of them. (You also had to demonstrate financial need. I had no problem doing that.) Then, when my second semester at the University ended, I was appointed to an editorial position on the campus newspaper, the University of Miami Hurricane. A small scholarship came with the responsibility. The academic scholarship covered my tuition. The journalism scholarship paid for my books. My mother didn't have to scrub floors.

But romance has a way of changing our lives. Late in the summer, still in Philadelphia, I fell in love.

I was going out with a young man who had no car, not unusual in the 1950's. After our third date, he suggested, "I have a friend who has a car. If you have a friend to introduce him to, we won't have to take the trolley on our next date." I called my cousin, Etta, who was exactly my age, my father's brother's daughter, and my friend as well as my cousin. She agreed to the blind date.

From the moment we saw each other, the new guy and I argued. His name was Al. Al wanted to play miniature golf. I was wearing a dress and high heels. I suggested a movie. We played miniature golf. I think we fought because it was a way of connecting. We were attracted to each other. He had piercing blue eyes, and his thick wavy hair was almost black.

A few days later, I was rushing down Market Street near City Hall in Philadelphia on my way from my summer job. I was in a hurry. I had a weekend date with a young man from home who had been drafted into the army and was stationed in Maryland. When he returned to his base, he wrote me a letter proposing marriage. Unfortunately for him, the wise guy standing in front of a jewelry store got in his way.

There he was, taking a five minute break from his summer job as I walked by. I stopped.

"I was going to call you," Al said, "but why should I get tied up with somebody who lives 1400 miles away when there are so many pretty girls in Philadelphia?"

We flirted with each other there on the street. He told me he'd call me after the weekend, then added, "Don't tell your cousin."

For the next three weeks, we saw each other every night. Each time, when he took me home, we stood in the dark doorway of my aunt and uncle's side entrance, making as much love as young people did in the innocence of the early 1950's. He begged me to get him invited to my friend's wedding in Newark, on September 23. Though I couldn't do that , I agreed to take a train back to Philadelphia after the wedding so that we could have another hour together before I flew to Miami.

The wedding was on a Sunday afternoon, and I took a six o'clock train out of Newark's Penn Station. Al met me at the train station in Philadelphia. We drove directly to the airport. My aunt and uncle met us there with my luggage.

We clung to each other like the young lovers we were, in front of my aunt and uncle. When Aunt Mildred got home, she quickly wrote a letter to Florence. "I think this is it," she wrote.

A month later, and it had been a long and lonely month for both of us, Al flew to Miami to propose to me.

It was Homecoming Weekend, always a special time on a college campus. On Friday evening, a few hours after I picked him up at the airport, we were sitting on the porch holding hands and I suggested we go to the Homecoming Dance at the University of Miami the next night. He didn't want to go to a dance. He didn't want to meet my friends. He wanted to be with me, just the two of us.

Sunday evening, my parents left us alone in the house. They must have taken Herbie with them, wherever they went. We had spent the afternoon driving to nowhere. I showed him the city, the university, my high school, and all he wanted was to look at me.

A few hours later, my parents still not home, he told me he was being drafted, that the next day, when he returned to Philadelphia, he had to report to the Draft Board. (As a part time college student, he wasn't eligible for a student deferment.)

"I brought you something," he told me. "It's not a ring. But if you take it, it will close the deal."

Nervous about proposing, desperate to cling to love and life, he used the language that came so easily to him, the salesman's language.

Before I could answer, my parents walked in the front door.

"Al just told me he's being drafted tomorrow," I blurted out.

They responded like the good people they were. They wished him luck. They hoped he would be safe, that the war would soon end. Then they walked into their bedroom and my mother said to my father, "Everybody always told me how smart Sissy is, and I never believed it. Now I see that it's true. She was smart enough not to tie herself up with a boy who is going into the army."

At that moment, I walked into their bedroom with my wrist extended. On it was a Bulova watch with several small diamonds on its face. "Look, Mom and Dad," I beamed, "Al and I are engaged!"

The next day, in Philadelphia, he passed an Army physical, and then a Navy physical examination. He was drafted into the United States Marine Corps.

The Marines, not for the first time in their history, augmented enlistments by participating in the draft. Marine casualties were so high at the battles of the Chosin Reservoir that enlistments were down.

The Army draftees were sent home and told to report the next day. The Marine Corps draftees were taken by bus to a Naval facility in Philadelphia, fed dinner, and told to call their families. Each draftee could make only one phone call. In a few hours, they would be on their way to Parris Island, South Carolina.

Their parents rushed to the railroad station, where they saw that their sons were behind a gated barrier. Soon, the gates were opened, and there were hugs and kisses of goodbye. The parents shuffled to their cars and trolleys, fighting back their tears and fears. Before long, the draftees boarded a train to Yamissee, South Carolina. At Yamissee, the Marine Corps buses, waiting for them, delivered them to Parris Island.

Now, every day I wrote letters to two young servicemen I loved — my brother, Norman, and my fiancé, Al.

The wise guy came back to me six weeks later a different man. He looked different. His wavy dark hair was replaced by a Marine Corps brush haircut. His broad shoulders were bony. His muscles were hard. He was too thin. But it wasn't his changed appearance that disturbed me the most. It was the meekness, the quiet. The *kibbitzer* had disappeared, replaced by a young man who had clearly been scared out of his skin by the legendary harsh training at Parris Island.

He wouldn't know, until he returned to Parris Island after this 10 day leave, what came next. He could soon be on his way to Korea.

He was posted to a new Marine Corps supply depot, in a place neither of us had ever heard of, Albany, Georgia.

In less than a year, I joined him there as his wife. The letter I sent to the University of Miami to give up my scholarship was typed on onion skin paper, a thin, cheap paper used for carbon copies. I have always regretted using that cheap paper, that I showed so little respect for the gift I had been given.

We were married on a cold and wet winter day in Philadelphia, December 28, 1952. Aunt Mildred took the place of my mother during the months we planned the wedding. She called her cousin, Eleanor, who had married a year or two earlier, and was as tall and slim as I was. She asked Eleanor if her niece, Sissy, could borrow her wedding gown. Of course! She and I went to the kosher catering halls in the city, and I signed a contract with the one she told me was best. Every Wednesday night, when the stores were open till 9:00 PM, we met in downtown Philadelphia (I was already there, at a job in a public relations agency), and she helped me choose a trousseau. She took me to a discount suit and coat store in South Philadelphia on a wintry Sunday, and convinced me to buy a soft pink, shag wool winter coat shaped like a pyramid for entirely too much money. She said it was a coat I would wear for years. She was right. I wore it through three pregnancies.

During the summers I was with Mildred and Lou, she and I often stood at an upstairs window on Sunday mornings, admiring the Black women passing by, neighbors and customers walking to church dressed in their Sunday finery. One of them, Mrs. Johnson, a dressmaker who lived across the street, always looked the most beautiful. Mildred asked Mrs. Johnson to make me two suits. My aunt had some fabric in a drawer, she told me. She probably made that up. She probably bought the fabric for me, and didn't want me to feel like a poor relative.

Mrs. Johnson made me two tailored suits, one in green wool, and one in gray wool.

Mildred, not my mother, was the woman who helped me with every decision I made.

I opened a savings account, and every week, I deposited most of my salary into the account to pay for the wedding. I wrote checks to the caterer and the band leader, the florist and the photographer, to the hotel where Al and I would spend our wedding night, and the hotel in Washington where we would stay the next two nights, before we drove to Georgia. I was not yet 20 years old.

Once, another uncle said to me, "I don't understand how your father can make you a wedding when he owes all of us money." I think I responded, "The same way you will make weddings for your daughters, dear uncle," or maybe I only wish I had said it.

Years later, Florence asked me if her brother, Lou, paid for my wedding. I told her that Mildred and Lou had always been very generous to me, and Norman sent me some of his Air Force paychecks. But I paid most of the wedding costs with the salary I earned in the six months before the wedding, when I worked at the public relations firm in Philadelphia and lived with my aunt and uncle.

Interference and Advice

The morning after the wedding, my new husband and I were interrupted by an early morning ring of the telephone in our hotel room. More asleep than awake, I answered the phone. Florence, my mother, was on the other end of the line.

"Are you Mrs. Carpey? Or Mrs. Carpey in name only?"

I mumbled, "I'm Mrs. Carpey."

She responded, "Are you all right?"

Only a daughter of Malka could have asked such a question of her newly married daughter. Only a granddaughter of Malka would have answered. We were used to such invasions of privacy.

Just a few years before my wedding, when my mother and I took the train to Philadelphia to my cousin Pearl's wedding, it turned out that we had return tickets on the same train that the newly married couple was taking to their honeymoon in Florida. I was pushed out of the seat next to my mother for several hours while she and Pearl whispered about the wedding night. The new husband was probably more embarrassed than I was. I knew there were no privacy barriers among the women in our family.

We, the first American born generation, sometimes laughed at their interference, sometimes resented it. I was about 15 when my mother walked into the bathroom while I sat on the toilet. Furious and embarrassed, I insisted that she was not to do this anymore. She must respect my privacy. She answered, "But I'm your mother! You don't have to hide anything from me."

Once, on a summer evening in Philadelphia, Malka happened to be in Mildred and Lou's house when a handsome, six foot tall young man came to see me. We had been together three or four times. We liked each other.

Malka looked him over, and asked, in her sweetest, friendliest voice, "Why aren't you in the army?"

He had been born with one arm shorter than the other, he told her, and showed her the arm in question. It was news to me. Though the U.S. Army had rejected him, the minor difference in length from shoulder to elbow in one arm didn't keep him from playing tennis, or being the good looking young man he was.

Bubbe smiled at him. The next morning, she called me on the telephone, and in her strongest voice, she ordered me not to date him anymore. "This boy is not for you. He is a cripple!"

I didn't marry him, but not because of my grandmother's order.

The *Knipple*

In the months before my wedding in Philadelphia, my grandmother called me one day to invite me to lunch at the Horn and Hardart restaurant on Market Street, near the department stores where she and her sisters often met to shop and spend a day together. She knew I worked just a few blocks away from the restaurant. When I got there, she was already at a table with her sister, Yetta.

Yetta and Malka, in their sixties, were considered old women at that time. But they never for a moment thought they were too old to give valuable advice to a young girl soon to be married. Especially a young girl who was one of their own.

As we sat and ate, they educated me, not about sex, but about money.

In Yiddish, Yetta instructed me on how to survive in a marriage. "Every woman needs her own *knipple*," she told me.

A *knipple* is a small piece you break off. When you are baking, you take a *knipple* of dough from the larger mound to roll out your cookies. I knew that Mema Yetta wasn't talking about cookies. She was teaching me that I had to have money of my own, my *knipple*, that no wife should have to ask permission from her husband to buy a dress for a family occasion, a gift for a child, a piece of jewelry now and then.

Today's *knipple* is often an independent checking account, but in 1950, few young women had money of their own.

A week after Al gave me an engagement ring, his parents invited the two families to a luncheon at a restaurant in Philadelphia. My parents flew to Philadelphia to meet Al's family and to participate in the celebration.

At the luncheon, my grandmother recognized an old friend from her first days in America. The friend's wife, who my grandmother had known, was long dead. Now, he was married to Al's aunt.

The next morning, Bubbe took one trolley, then another, to visit her old friend at his jewelry store in a neighborhood called Kensington. "Nathan," she asked him, "what kind of a family is my granddaughter marrying into? Are they fine people?"

He assured her that they were. My grandmother was only doing her job, using her contacts to research the background of a family that would soon be mine. In her eyes, it was her right and responsibility. But Al and his family didn't think so when Uncle Nathan told them about her visit.

Seventeen — Family Togetherness

My parents didn't bring Herbie with them when they flew from Miami to Philadelphia that December for my wedding. He stayed with a neighbor for those few days. My little brother, who was 14 that winter, could not tolerate the winter winds and freezing temperatures. They didn't bring him with them when I got engaged, either, though that was the June before the wedding, when the weather was as warm as a Florida June.

Only later, years later, did it occur to me that they may have left Herbie home because they were hiding something they could not face. They were hiding the truth not only from their relatives, and maybe from my new in-laws, but also from themselves.

Less than a year later, when Herbie was 15, the school counselor called my mother for the first time. She recommended that my mother meet with a psychologist at the University of Miami, that my brother be tested by this psychologist. I was in Georgia with my Marine husband. Norman, still in the Air Force, was in Los Alamos. We both got the same hysterical letter from our mother. The psychologist told her our brother was retarded.[8]

"He'll always be the way he is now," the psychologist said.

Norman called me, and we agreed that the psychologist was crazy. Our little brother was immature for his age, but surely he was a normal kid. We both wrote long, denying, positive letters to our parents.

Our brother could not only read, though not very well, but he knew as much about baseball as any sportscaster. And he had a terrific sense of direction. When the relatives came from Philadelphia, it was our little brother, Herbie, who took them on buses and guided them to their destinations. What he wanted to remember, he remembered, Norman and I agreed.

But the psychologist's tests did not lie.

When Herbie turned 16, the school system's legal responsibility ended. He had never been to a special class. He had never received any vocational training. My parents were never offered any counseling. Somehow, my mother was steered to a trade school. He made a bookcase and a stool. He never made anything else.

In October, 1955, in Philadelphia, I gave birth to our first child, our daughter Jodi. A month earlier, Florence and Sam came back to Philadelphia to live. They wanted to be part of their grandchild's life. Now, they were willing to take a chance on Herbie's survival in the winter winds. Perhaps they thought they had sacrificed enough for him. Perhaps they were tired of pretending, even to each other.

They picked up the extended family life as if they had never left it. The women began every day on the phone with each other. Ida and Ben lived a few short blocks from their daughter, Pearl, and their grandchildren. My

8 The word "retarded" was used at the time to describe a person now referred to as "developmentally disabled."

parents lived around the corner from me. Our small row houses were often filled with aunts and cousins and their children. I had three children in five years. So did most of my cousins, both on my mother's and my father's side of the family.

Sometimes, there was an overabundance of family togetherness. And there was always an undercurrent of rivalry. I hated Mother's Day. Malka was the primary mother. "*Ich bin da Momma*," meant the same in her old age as it had when she was the pampered wife of Goddel in the *shtetl*. She came first. We dressed our little ones in their holiday finery and drove the 15 minutes to Bubbe's house, with gifts in our hands. Everyone assembled there at the same time, all the generations of the family. We tasted the goodies she had cooked and baked. We lined the little ones up to take family photos with their grandparents and great grandparents. It was as if Mother's Day was a Jewish holiday. Malka adopted it as one.

Our next stop was to Al's parents, where we made the customary Mother's Day visit, presented the gift, spent an hour being respectful and taking more photos.

By the time we got to Florence's house, the kids were cranky and tired, and so were we.

We didn't know how lucky we were.

EIGHTEEN — OUR LOST AND FOUND AUNT

IN THE SUMMER OF 1965, when Aunt Frayda came, her sisters and brothers were no longer living "behind the store," the grocery stores, the butcher shops, the dry cleaners. Though they were still storekeepers, they drove to their stores in the morning, and came home at night to their own homes, some with more than one bathroom. The end of the Depression and the prosperity that came with World War Two had lifted our parents' generation, her generation, several rungs up the economic ladder.

What had our aunt's life been like? What had her children's lives been like? We would soon learn. But not too soon. It would be a long time before Aunt Frayda allowed her barriers to fall away, before we got glimpses of the life that might have been ours.

At first, my aunt told us only the good things. She gave us gifts. New chrome *samovars*, poor copies of the brass *samovars* some of our great aunts brought with them when they left the old country. Brightly painted ceramic dolls from the Ukraine, shaped like eggs that fit into each other. Beautifully embroidered hats from Uzbekistan. Miniature cups and saucers. Later, when there was some small trade between the Soviet Union and the United States, at the beginning of the Soviet Jewry exodus to the United States and Israel, we would see the ceramic dolls everywhere—in toy stores and craft shows, even at the dollar stores in our neighborhoods. We learned that they had a name. They were *matroshkas,* hand painted crafts made by Ukrainian women. The beautifully embroidered, intricately cross-stitched, and brightly colored caps were *yarmulkes* worn by the Bukharan Jews who had been in Uzbekistan hundreds of years before my aunt and the other Russian Jews who settled in Tashkent after the Soviet Revolution.

We were as ignorant of her land as she was of ours.

When Aunt Frayda gave us these gifts, we understood, without being told, that it had not been easy for her to find gifts for us, nor to pay for them.

In my cousin's Cadillac, on the drive from Kennedy Airport to Philadelphia, she had responded, "*Meir habben dus echad*" (We have this also), when her brothers and sisters pointed out the American highways and bridges to her.

Every American wonder we showed her brought the same response. "*Meir habben dus echad.*" We didn't believe her. We knew she had spent several days in Moscow before her flight to New York. We were certain she had been tutored by the Soviet authorities, and told that "we have this, also" was to be her response to everything she saw in America.

On my aunt's first morning with us, I drove my mother to my grandmother's house after I got my children off to school.

Mother and daughter were sitting at my grandmother's kitchen table when we arrived, talking to each other in the Yiddish I understood, but was hardly fluent in. I spoke a pidgin Yiddish when Aunt Frayda arrived. After she had been with us a few weeks, I could talk all day in the Yiddish I had heard all my life, and now had to get out of my mouth.

That morning in the kitchen, they kept touching each other. My grandmother's hand was in her daughter's hair, or patting her arm. Their eyes didn't stray from each other. My grandmother started every sentence with, "Daughter, mine" and my aunt started her responses with "Momma." The sound of those ordinary words coming from their lips made me hold back tears.

They looked like sisters, not mother and daughter. My aunt looked like the older sister. Her gray– white hair was pulled away from her face in a bun. She wore a shapeless dress that covered her heavy, square body from her neck to her ankles. Her features were beautiful. The dark brown eyes had sparks of gold in them, so much like my mother's eyes. She had the same small, well shaped nose as my two uncles, her brothers. Her hands were my mother's hands. Every exposed part of her was rough, over worn, uncared for. You didn't have to be told that her life had been harder than we could imagine.

My grandmother, on the other hand, was a woman who had always been taken care of, first by her husband, then by her children. When my cousins and I were growing up, Uncle Lou often told us, "You are all pretty girls, but your grandmother was more beautiful than all of you."

On that morning, the morning of my aunt's first full day in her mother's home in America, none of us could imagine the constant activity and excitement of the next several months. Second and third cousins came from Boston and Baltimore, from Florida and Tennessee, to participate in the family drama. We all shared the same history. We, like Frayda, were the descendants of Itzak and Esther. We had grown up with the stories of the *shtetl*, and, though the family ties had stretched thin through the generations, the miracle of Frayda's visit brought us together. Everybody gave parties, made dinners, took photos.

But first, she had to get to know her family again. She and her mother and my mother and aunts sat at the kitchen table and talked. "Momma, why did you leave me?" she asked. And the response, "Daughter, mine, what could I do? They would have killed us all. I thought you would follow when the child was older."

In the beginning, each told the other only what they wanted the other to know about their lives. In those first weeks, she didn't tell us about the Stalin years, or the years of famine and five year plans. She waited until much later to tell us about the cold, hard years in Siberia.

She was proud to show us photos of her daughter, the pediatrician, and her family. Only months later did she say to me, as she fingered my inexpensive straw handbag, "Oh, if only my Zena could have a bag like this for her medical instruments." Her daughter's medical bag was a paper bag.

Once, she watched me open a container of frozen orange juice in winter. As I added the cans of water and filled my pitcher, she said to me, "Child, do you know how fortunate you are to be able to give your babies fresh orange juice? The vitamins! So good for your children's health."

She walked into our modest houses and saw palaces. "A baby in a crib has a room of his own! I never saw such a thing."

She tried very hard not to make these comments. She tried to keep up the refrain of "*Meir habben dus echad.*" We have this, also.

Slowly, she became more comfortable, and more open. Once, she and I walked through the aisles of a department store. She stopped at the furniture department and began play acting. If she could, she told me, she would choose this dining room table. And these chairs. How nice it would be to have chairs that matched.

The first time we took her to a supermarket, she was almost blinded by the full and plenty. It was impossible for her to hide her response. Fresh oranges piled up for the picking, and never out of season. Fruits and vegetables and milk and bread. Whole sections of beef and chickens. Never a counter empty of food.

She didn't like everything about America, especially the waste, and in 1965, Americans did not recycle. She couldn't stand the way we threw glass containers into the trash when they could be used again.

Once, when she and I were leaving the supermarket, a boy who looked about 15 helped me load my car. I handed him a tip, and thanked him. She disapproved. "Giving a child money teaches him that there is a way to get money even if he doesn't work hard in school," she told me. "This is not good. He must have a good education. He must spend his time studying, so that he will qualify for a profession."

Sometimes, she saw the full and plenty of the American life as an excess.

One day, she visited the family of the only cousin she had known in the *shtetl*, Frima's oldest son, Israel, who became Irv in America. Frayda, sitting in the bedroom of Israel's teen-aged daughter, Arlene, was shocked at the disorder and overabundance of a typical American girl's bedroom. Arlene remembers the overflowing, open drawers filled with carelessly rolled sweaters, many of them cashmere, too many to count, none of them neatly folded.

Frayda openly disapproved of the carelessness of the young girl. Why did her parents permit such disarray?

Arlene, telling me this story, remembers that Frayda had a "terrible skin rash."

I respond that Frayda had psoriasis, and that when she returned to Tashkent, we continued to send her medicine for her psoriasis for many years.

"I have psoriasis," says Arlene, now a middle aged woman who keeps her bureau drawers in order.

"So does my brother," I tell her. "It runs in the family."

When Frayda had been with us for about a month, my father and mother visited her on a Saturday morning at my grandmother's house, then brought her to their home for a few days. My parents didn't notice the police car behind them. They were so busy telling my aunt family stories that they didn't realize that Frayda sat silently in the back seat of the car. When they were almost home, the police car made a turn away from them, and then my aunt confessed her fear. She thought the police were after them. She had been terrified during the whole ride.

"No, no," said my father. "This is America. In America, the police just don't come to take you away."

Frayda, left, and Florence, right, in front of Florence's row
house in Philadelphia shortly after Frayda's arrival.

Part of the Family at Last

Within a few days of their reunion, Malka took her daughter
to the beauty shop and instructed the hairdresser to get
rid of Frayda's old lady bun. Frayda sat still, grateful for
the maternal attention. Hours later, Frayda's thick gray
hair, its drabness brightened with a "rinse," framed her
face. Soon, Frayda had an American wardrobe, chosen
by her mother, happily paid for by her brothers and their
wives.

She was invited to a wedding in Miami Beach in September. The bride, Barbara, was the great granddaughter of Itzak and Esther of the *shtetl* of Sobolifka in the Ukraine, just as I was, just as Frayda's two children were. The bride's grandmother was my bubbe's long dead, older sister, Channa. During my years in Miami, Barbara was a little girl and I was her babysitter. Her parents, Blanche and Sol, younger than my parents, were the ones I went to when I had a question about sex. I remember once asking them, "Are you supposed to move when you have sex?"

"Honey," said Blanche, in her soft Southern drawl (they were part of the Nashville and Baltimore branch of the family), "it's a lot more fun if you do."

Malka and Frima, the only two of their generation still living, were invited to every wedding and bar mitzvah in the extended family, and now, Frayda boarded a plane to Miami with them to meet the descendants of the aunt she remembered from her childhood. She blinked at the glitter and gold of Miami Beach.

The wedding took place at the Algiers Hotel on Labor Day. It was hurricane season. The day after the wedding, the wedding guests woke up to 100 mile an hour winds, a hotel with no electricity and no operating toilets. A major hurricane kept the glitzy hotel dark for several days. The roaring wind and rain made the hotel guests prisoners to nature.

My grandmother, Malka, and her sister, Frima, who were together in the worst of times in the Ukraine, wrung their hands and were frightened. They complained, like Americans accustomed to creature comforts, about the lack of water and food, the toilets that didn't flush, wind, rain, the darkness.

Frayda, on the other hand, took it all in stride. She had been through worse. She took care of the two old women and their husbands until the lights went on and the winds died down and the toilets flushed.

A month later, in October, 1965, with her mother beside her, she walked into Beth Sholom Synagogue, in Elkins Park, Pennsylvania, to attend the bar mitzvah of the grandson of her sister, Ida. Beth Sholom has the distinction of being the only synagogue in the world designed by the famous architect, Frank Lloyd Wright.

Frayda sat in the front row of the magnificent synagogue, her mother beside her, surrounded by her brothers and sisters and their spouses and children. The traditional Saturday morning service unfolded, and the bar mitzvah boy, David, read from the ancient Torah. It was the first time she had been in a synagogue in half a century. She lived in a culture and country that believed religion was the "opiate of the masses." Her children and grandchildren, though they knew they were Jews, had never been to *shul*. Perhaps she thought the whole thing was foolish, a childish tradition for people who were ignorant enough to believe in a God. Perhaps she connected with the religion of her childhood, when her grandfather, Itzak *stolyar*, and her father, Goddel, went to *shul* every Sabbath, and the women and girls were upstairs, behind the *mechitze* that separated them from the men, and the rhythm of their lives was defined by the Hebrew calendar.

David's bar mitzvah party continued with a dinner dance that evening. Back to the famous synagogue we all went. The band played till late in the night. The food and drink kept coming. It was a bar mitzvah party Philip Roth could have written about.

In David's bar mitzvah album, there are two priceless photographs. In one, Frayda is dancing a *freilich*, a circle dance, with her brothers and sisters, a look of disbelief on her face.

The other photo is the formal family photograph. The grandparents of the bar mitzvah boy, Ida and Ben, are in the middle, surrounded by my grandmother and her husband Philip, and Ida's sisters and brothers and their spouses. These are the only family photos that include all five of Malka's children.

Malka and her five children. Standing, left to right, Charles, Doris, Ben, Sam, Florence, Frayda, Mildred. Seated, left to right, Ida, Philip and Malka, Lou.

Another Sad Farewell and a New Beginning

Too soon, it was time for Frayda to leave us. The day came when mother and daughter clung together for a last embrace, when the parties ended and the tears began. She had been with us six months. She was ready to return to her husband and children and grandchildren in Tashkent. On both sides of the world, we were grateful for the gift of love, of family connection. And we were certain we would never see each other again.

But life has a way of surprising us.

Once, early in her visit, I told my aunt that when I was a teenager, my parents were afraid I would leave them to be a pioneer on a *kibbutz* in Israel. I told her I had danced in the streets of Miami Beach in 1948, when the State of Israel was declared, that all my life, I had been a Zionist. She turned away from me, pale with fear. "You are a Zionist? Do not tell me any more."

Who could believe that less than 10 years after her return to Tashkent, her own daughter, Zena, would be one of the thousands of Soviet Jews who were permitted to leave the Soviet Union to live in Israel? Zena and her husband, David, and two sons arrived in Israel in the first wave of emigration from the Soviet Union.

But history threatened to repeat itself. When Zena left the Soviet Union, her mother remained in Tashkent, and so did Zena's daughter, Anna, with her husband, Grisha. Frayda's husband, David, had died earlier.

When they kissed goodbye, the mothers and their daughters were haunted by the past. This time, though, the gods and the governments were kinder. Frayda and her daughter, Zena, and her granddaughter, Anna, along with their husbands and children, were soon together in Israel. Later, Frayda's son, Golya, and his extended family also were permitted to leave Tashkent to settle in Israel.

NINETEEN — A DAUGHTER FOUND, A DAUGHTER LOST

MY MOTHER, FLORENCE, WAS THE first of her generation to die. In September, 1971, a few days before the Rosh Hashanah holiday, she suffered a massive heart attack. I was no longer around the corner. A year earlier, we had moved to a much larger house in a new suburb, an hour's car ride away.

My son, Daniel, would be 13 that June. We had already made arrangements for his bar mitzvah party. He was already studying his portion of the Torah.

From September to June, my mother labored to live. She died three weeks before my son's bar mitzvah.

During those terrible months, I spent most of my time at her side, in the hospital or in her home. Each morning, as soon as my children's school bus arrived, I hurried to my car and began the hour's journey through city traffic.

Malka stood with me at her daughter's hospital bed and endured the unthinkable—watching her child die. My aunts and uncles and cousins took turns sitting with us. Still, there were many afternoons when only Malka and I sat together. Often, I would drive her home. On one of those days, she insisted, "Sissy, come up to my apartment and take some cookies to your children. I baked yesterday."

So instead of leaving her in the lobby of the apartment building and continuing on my way home, I accompanied her to the apartment. Then, she insisted on making me a cup of tea. She brought out her cookie jar. "Look at this," she said, admiring her handiwork. I don't remember what she had baked, or if she was also packing other food for me to take home. I only remember that my children were waiting for me and that I had spent months watching my mother die and now I was expected to admire my grandmother's artistry in the kitchen.

For the first time, I blew up at her. "Bubbe," I cried, as the tears ran down my cheeks, "I have to go home to my children. Let me go!"

"Oh, my child," she exclaimed. "I only wanted to help you, to give you dinner to take home to your family."

My mother's funeral was on Mother's Day, 1972.

The *shiva* was at my house. For a week, the house was filled with family. My father and my brothers slept in our house. My aunts and uncles took the hour's car ride to my home every day to observe the week of mourning with me, as one family. My grandmother, too, sat with us, mourning the loss of her child. In the evening, everybody showed up, sisters-in-law and brothers-in-law of everyone, neighbors and friends from long ago or not, cousins and more cousins.

As a daughter observing the week of mourning, I was not supposed to do any work. But I had no choice but to start each day with a vacuum cleaner in my hand, as I dusted and straightened up and cleaned bathrooms, getting ready for the day's onslaught. Every night, there was a *minyan* in my family room, the traditional evening service during which the mourning family says *kaddish*. The rabbi came. The house filled up with men and women from the synagogue who passed around prayer books and paid their respects to us, the mourners. Every few hours all week, the doorbell rang and a delivery man brought dinner to my house, trays of cooked food, towers of fresh fruit and cookies, all sent by friends and relatives as an expression of their love and caring.

One evening, as I walked upstairs to have a moment with my children, I came upon Aunt Doris giving a friend of hers a tour of my home. She was in my bedroom, showing off the oversized closet, as big as a baby's nursery had been in my first house. I was embarrassed, not because Aunt Doris was showing a stranger my intimate bedroom, but because the closet in question was a jumbled mess. I had spent the last nine months watching my mother die, not organizing closets. I gave the two women a quick smile, and walked across the hallway to my two boys, Stuart, 20 months younger than his brother, and Danny, the bar mitzvah boy. I spent a few moments checking their homework, hugged them both, and spent a few moments alone with my daughter, Jodi, who had turned sixteen the week of her grandmother's heart attack.

When the mourning period ended, I took to my bed. My tricky back went out. I couldn't straighten up.

In the same week, I got a call from the owner of the shop where I had ordered the dress I expected to wear at my son's bar mitzvah. "I have bad news," he told me, "The dress you ordered won't arrive in time for your son's bar mitzvah."

"That's not bad news," I responded. "My mother died last week."

At the bar mitzvah, I sat next to my son on the first row of the synagogue with my husband and our daughter and younger son. The family, grandparents, aunts and uncles and cousins, filled the rows behind us.

When the Torah service began, my father was the first one called to recite the blessing before the Torah was read. That morning, before we left for the synagogue, he had placed my mother's engagement ring on my finger. Neither of us could cry. Neither of us could talk.

Now, as my father chanted the familiar blessing in Hebrew, his voice broke. He struggled to compose himself. Danny, seeing his grandfather's contorted face, began crying silently. In just a few minutes, my son would be called to the Torah for the first time in his life. He would chant the portion he had practiced for so many months while his grandmother lay dying. Many times, I brought him with me to her house, where she lay in a hospital bed in the same dining room where, before the heart attack, she had served us hundreds of Friday night and holiday dinners. He sat by her hospital bed and chanted his Torah portion for her. He modeled the suit he would wear, his first suit.

Now, I held on to his hand. Then, behind me, I heard the crackle of cellophane paper. It was Aunt Doris rummaging through her pocketbook. She brought out a handful of hard candies and handed them to my son. He popped one, then another, into his mouth. The sweetness of the candy helped him regain his control.

Later, when the service ended, and Danny had read his portion so beautifully, it was time to take congratulations, to walk into the bar mitzvah party in the adjoining room of the synagogue.

Malka walked toward me. Our eyes met, then we looked away. She put her arm through mine, and looked straight into my eyes once more. And she said, "You and me, Sissy, we must be *ladies*."

I knew what she meant. If she, the mother of Florence, or I, the daughter of Florence, broke down, my son's bar mitzvah party would be a wake, not a celebration.

We almost danced into the room, wide smiles on our faces, determined to celebrate life, and a child's rite of passage.

TWENTY — FAMILY CIRCLE—1975

IT WAS OUR FIRST COUSINS Club.

Months earlier, there were two deaths in the family in the same week. At the first funeral, the rabbi had to work very hard to get our attention so that he could start the funeral service of our great uncle. The buzz of conversation among cousins twice removed and three times removed, who had never known those terms when they were children, filled the funeral parlor. Each branch of the family was bringing the others up to date on new babies, college–bound children, and marriages. One of my cousins took a giant leap across an aisle to give me a bear hug. Once, he and I had gone out on double dates. Now, we saw each other only at family funerals.

The rabbi finally succeeded in directing our attention to our uncle in his casket.

At the second funeral, as we gathered on the steps of the same funeral parlor, the cousins looked at each other and said, "This is ridiculous. We only see each other at funerals. What has happened to the family?"

The American born generations had prospered. We lived in houses an hour's drive from the row houses and "dwellings" behind the grocery stores and candy stores and butcher shops. Though our dining rooms were large enough to hold more relatives, we had lost the habit of being together. We had friends who were closer to us than family.

My grandmother's prophecy was fulfilled. "In America," Malka often said, "*Fremda menschen* mean more than family."

The Yiddish phrase, *fremda menschen,* though it may sound like "friendly people," translates as "strangers," "outsiders." In her later years, Malka went to family weddings and bar mitzvahs where the *fremda menschen* outnumbered the family. She came home angry. Who were these people who took the place of her sisters' children and grandchildren at the tables of the catered affairs? Who were these strangers?

We decided to start a Cousins Club. Invitations were sent to cousins none of us had ever met. We knew only that they were sons and daughters of other cousins. Some lived in places none of us had visited, connected to the family only by the past. More than 100 people responded with a dinner reservation and a check.

On the day of the reunion, we sat the college students together, and the rest of us beamed as the youngest generation of Itzak *stolyar's kinder,* the great-grandchildren of our immigrant aunts, got to know each other.

Soon, the room was alive with the sounds of family, some of us speaking in the shorthand of our past. Then, from every corner of the room came the shouts, "Mema Malka, say a few words to us!"

My bubbe, the last of her generation, slowly walked to the front of the room.

The crowd silenced. Malka, frail and ancient, looked around the room, at the faces that reminded her of her sisters, at the little ones and the college students, all of them connected to her by blood.

Then, in the Yiddish that the youngest generations did not understand, she said, "If only my sisters were here, to see what a beautiful *meshpucha* (family) you are. Stay together, my children, because there is nothing more important than family."

She paused. Then she said, "I only ask of you one thing." All eyes were on her. The room was silent, the better to hear her voice.

"Promise me that you will all come to my funeral."

We erupted in laughter, and rushed to encircle her.

An hour later, when the desserts were served and the room quieted down, Cousin Raymond, the grandson of my bubbe's sister, Inda, the same Inda who had organized the young girls of the *shtetl* to craft a new *chuppa*, went to the front of the room. He had, earlier, put up a movie screen.

He and his wife, Beverly, had just returned from a year's study in Israel. There, he met Frayda's daughter, Zena. The young couple spent many evenings with the new immigrants to Israel, who welcomed the friendship of their American cousins. Ray and Beverly brought their movies from Israel to our family gathering.

In a few moments, the silent screen was alive.

Malka walked up to the screen and stood before it, leaning on her cane. She stared at Frayda's daughter, as frame after frame of the granddaughter she would never know passed before her aged eyes. There wasn't a sound in the room.

Twenty One — Full Circle

Israel—1977

I⊤ WAS ALMOST MIDNIGHT WHEN we arrived at Ben Gurion Airport in Tel Aviv a few days before the Passover Seder in 1977. My husband, Al, and I were weary and short tempered.

Months earlier, he had come home with news of a business conference in Amsterdam in the spring. Would I go with him? Only if we flew to Israel after we left Amsterdam, I replied. I wanted to meet Frayda's daughter, Zena, and her family. He wasn't pleased with my response. But I persisted. No Israel? No Amsterdam.

I wrote a letter, in English, to my cousin Zena, telling her when we would arrive at Ben Gurion Airport, that we had signed up for a tour of Israel, and that I was eager to meet her. We would be in Haifa for a few days, and I knew that Kiryat Yam, where she lived, was a suburb of Haifa.

She never responded to my letter. I told myself that she was new to the land. She was learning Hebrew, not English. My tour guide would help me find her when the tour stopped in Haifa.

On our last evening in Amsterdam, Al, never a relaxed flyer, decided he was sick. He had a cold, a virus. He was tired. He had seen enough. It was time to go home. He suggested we call the airlines and cancel our morning flights. There were two of them, Amsterdam to Rome, and Rome to Tel Aviv.

I told him he could go home if he wanted to. I was going to Israel.

In the early morning, the two of us, tired and short tempered with each other, made our way to the Amsterdam Airport and boarded the plane to Rome. It was an easy flight. I think we fell asleep.

The tough stuff started at the Rome Airport.

We were on our own once we got off that first airplane. We waited forever for our much too heavy luggage, while the sounds coming from the airport loudspeakers were all in the language of Italy. The airport was large. Nobody spoke English. Nobody directed us to the boarding gate of our El Al plane. The porters ignored us. Al piled our heaviest suitcases on his shoulders and I walked behind him, weighed down with my load, both of us stopping to ask strangers, some who were airport employees, to direct us to our plane. No one understood us. No one took a minute to help us. It was a traveler's nightmare.

Now, we were angry with each other, Al muttering that he knew we should have gone home from Amsterdam, I stopping more strangers as we almost ran through the airport with our heavy luggage weighing us down. Then, like a sudden sunrise, the El Al gate was in front of us. And the seats were filled with all the people who would soon board the plane with us. We hadn't missed our flight.

Exhausted, and still annoyed with each other, we took the only two vacant seats in the waiting area, on different rows. A well dressed Italian man, seated beside me, smiled at me when I sat down, and in his beautiful Italian accent, said, "Travel is hard, but wonderful."

Every moment on that flight to Israel was an emotional high for me. I, who had danced in the streets of Miami Beach when the United Nations voted "yes" to the establishment of the Jewish state, I, who my immigrant parents feared would leave them to become a Zionist settler on a *kibbutz*, was wide eyed and alert through the entire flight. The stewardesses welcomed us in Hebrew, then in English and other languages. The pilot in the cockpit did the same. At the back of the plane, a group of Orthodox Jews, with their prayer books open and their bodies swaying, loudly chanted the evening prayers, and none of the other passengers seemed annoyed or disapproving. The stewardesses offered us only kosher dinners. The signs and the sounds of the Hebrew language were all around me.

Al and I relaxed. He napped. And soon, our plane landed at Ben Gurion Airport in Tel Aviv.

We had left Amsterdam early in the morning. Now, it felt and looked like midnight. The airport was empty, except for the people getting off our plane. As we went through Customs, I noticed, for the first time, that we had flown to Israel with at least a dozen Soviet Jews. I felt emotionally connected to them, not only because of my family's history, but because I hoped to meet my own Soviet Jews, my cousin Zena and her family, when our tour stopped in Haifa.

There were too few porters in the airport, and even fewer taxis outside. We gathered our suitcases and ran into the street in front of the airport and stood there until we caught the attention of one of the scarce cab drivers. Actually, I stood there while my husband ran after the cabs until one driver paid attention to him and stopped.

I remembered the words of the man in the Rome airport. "Travel is hard, but wonderful." Soon, I would remember the words of my grandmother, Malka, when I came to her house a few days before the trip. "May your days be filled with flowers," she said.

The cab driver drove us to our hotel in Tel Aviv.

The two of us dragged our tired bodies and our luggage into the hotel and to the registration desk. It took only a few moments to sign in, get our room key from the one person on duty, and walk toward the elevator with our bags. I don't remember when I felt the presence of people walking behind us. I ignored them, as anyone would ignore the presence of strangers behind them walking toward the same elevator. I heard them whisper to each other. We were in front of the elevator when I heard a woman's soft voice, barely whispering my name, "Sissy." It was almost a question. I didn't process it. "Sissy," once more.

Suddenly, I knew. I turned and looked into my own face. "Zena," I cried, and I fell into the arms of the cousin I had never known, a granddaughter of Malka, a great granddaughter of Itzak and Esther of the *shtetl* of Sobolifka. She was carrying a bouquet of flowers.

She and her husband and their 16–year–old son had been waiting for hours. The hotel reception staff knew they were waiting for us. When we checked in, the man on duty signaled that we were their relatives, and they began their walk behind us.

For the next four hours, we sat on the bed and the chairs in our hotel room and talked and talked and talked — in Yiddish. We laughed. We listened to each other's stories. We fell in love with each other. My husband and I were no longer weary travelers. My cousin and I would never again be strangers to each other.

"What time in the morning will you be ready to come to our home?" Zena and her husband, David, wanted to know. "We will come here in our car and drive you to our home, and we will spend the *Shabbat* together."

They were staying overnight in Tel Aviv, with David's cousins.

We explained that our tour started early Sunday morning. The bus would be at the hotel at 9:00AM.

"Of course," said David. "I will drive you back here Sunday morning."

We held up our tour bus on Sunday morning. It was a long ride from Kiryat Yam to the hotel in Tel Aviv. Our fellow tourists did not welcome us with friendly smiles when we caught up with the bus. But all day Saturday, in Kiryat Yam, the Soviet newcomers to Israel who were our cousins' friends kissed us and danced with us and brought us bouquets of flowers.

Zena and Sissy: The daughters of sisters, strangers to each other until they met in Israel. Photo taken in the author's back yard, when Zena came to meet her American family.

New York—2007

My beautiful, blonde cousin, Pearl, was struck with multiple sclerosis when she was in her early 40's. Pearl and I, the daughters of sisters, lived near each other when our children were born. We often met for breakfast at a local pancake house with our babies and toddlers in tow. In those years, we lived in small row houses, our parents only a block away. None of us had a dining room big enough to seat the extended family. I went to my parents' house for the holiday dinners. Pearl went to her parents' house.

The children grew up. We prospered. We moved to larger houses in suburbs an hour away from each other. Pearl and I talked on the phone almost every day, but our children barely knew each other.

Soon, Pearl and I were grandmothers. I baked cookies for my grandchildren, made the chicken soup they loved, and filled my home with their photos and art work. Pearl lay in a nursing home.

She had been in the nursing home several years when I convinced her husband and children to come to our family Passover Seder. Our sons and daughters, now parents themselves, didn't remember the days when they sat in high chairs at those pancake houses when Pearl and I spoke to each other in the shorthand of family. Now, before the Seder began, I sat back and listened to the buzz of conversation among my adult children and Pearl's adult children.

Then I noticed that my granddaughter, Rachel, and Pearl's granddaughter, Alex, were ignoring each other. They were strangers. They were shy. I decided not to interfere.

Years went by. Rachel and Alex didn't cross paths.

Beautiful Pearl died in the nursing home. On a cold winter day in 2007, the family gathered at the cemetery, just a few of us, Pearl and Morrie's children and grandchildren, a few cousins, her brother, who flew in from Phoenix.

After the burial, we went to the home she had shared with Morrie. We did what people do after a funeral. We ate. We talked. We shared our memories. I filled a plate with food and sat down next to the young woman I had last seen when she was nine or ten, when she came to my house for the Seder.

"So, Alex," I asked, "What are you doing now?" She told me she lived in New York and liked her job, and, yes, she loved New York. "Oh," I said, "My granddaughter is in New York, too." And I gave her Rachel's name.

"Omigod," she almost shouted, a look of shock on her face. "Rachel is my cousin?"

In New York a few years earlier, Alex lived across the hall from a friend of Rachel's at New York University. They did not get to know each other and had no clue they were cousins, but said a friendly hello when their paths crossed. Little did they imagine that they were both named for my mother and carried the same Hebrew name. Family trees were not part of their conversations. And neither remembered the other from that awkward meeting at the Passover Seder at my house when they were little girls.

After the funeral, the two young women emailed each other, "We're cousins!" Since then, they've built a close relationship, and are part of each other's lives. One evening, while out for a drink in New York, Rachel noticed that Alex was wearing a cameo ring. "I have a ring just like that," she told Alex. They both wear the cameo rings that once belonged to their great grandmothers, the sisters, Ida and Florence, who must be smiling somewhere at the miracle of their great granddaughters' friendship.

EPILOGUE — 2009

DURING THE SOVIET JEWRY MOVEMENT, and the great immigration of Russian Jews to Israel and America, all of our lost relatives settled in Israel.

After several years in Israel, two branches of the lost and found family moved once more, this time to Toronto, Canada. They are Zena's older son, Yossi, his wife, Chaya and their children, and Zena's grandson, Michael, and his family. We have attended Yossi's sons' bar mitzvahs in Toronto, and have been welcomed as family by Michael and his wife, Danna, and their two little boys.

Yossi and Chaya are the only branch of the descendents of Itzak and Esther of the *shtetl* of Sobolifa who have returned to the Orthodox Judaism of their ancestors. Once, shortly after Yossi and Chaya immigrated to Canada, he asked me if I knew the name of the *rebbe* the Jews of Sobolifka followed. I called my older cousins. None of them knew more than I did.

Though many of our parents were story tellers, this was one bit of history they left out. They were raising American children.

On our most recent trip to Toronto, I brought a photograph of my grandmother dressed for a family event in a long silk gown, her silver hair piled high in a mountain of curls, as if she were a young woman. The photo was taken at her youngest grandson's bar mitzvah party, when she was in her late 70's. I gave the photograph to the only descendant of Malka who carries her name, her great great granddaughter, Yossi and Chaya's daughter, Malka.

Zena and I call each other regularly, and still struggle with the Yiddish that is our only common language. We cannot make up for the lost years. Still, we try to nurture the family ties.

We try to nurture the family ties in America, also. The Cousins Club reunions of the American—born family only lasted a few years. Sometimes, we, the first American generation, meet by chance on a street in Philadelphia, at a concert, or a lecture. We take small photos from our wallets and brag about our grandchildren and promise to meet for dinner.

The generations after us are mostly strangers to each other, as each family tree gets wider and longer, and too few know that they are descended from Itzak and Esther of the *shtetl* of Sobolifka in the province of Podolia in the Ukraine.

And yet, sometimes, they find each other and become friends.

It happened to Zena and me. It happened to Rachel and Alex.

It is as if there is an invisible force pulling us towards each other, encouraging us to become intertwined in each other's lives. And generations from now, perhaps these connections will make our roots stronger, as the family continues to tell the stories of Malka and her children.

APPENDIX

A photo from the *shtetl*: Israel, left, Frima, and the baby boy who died shortly after this photo was taken.

FOLLOWING IS A TRANSCRIPTION OF a hand written memoir given to me by my cousin, Israel Bogdonoff. In America, he was sometimes "Izzy," and sometimes "Irving." Izzy's mother was Frima, who was Malka's youngest sister.

I had learned of my cousin's memoir from his younger brothers, Morris and Philip, both of whom were born in Philadelphia. Their older brother was born in Sobolifka, and had played with my mother and her sisters and brothers during the few peaceful moments of their common childhood. He was in his 80's when he wrote this memoir.

When I called him, and asked to see what he had written, he was not enthusiastic. Now, as I sat across from him at yet another tiny, round kitchen table, I understood his hesitance. First, we shared a cookie, a cup of tea, and made small talk about the family. Then, his manuscript in front of him, he said, "I'm going to read this to you. You see, I never had much schooling, and my spelling and grammar are not good."

Realizing he was embarrassed, I turned on my tape recorder and opened my notebook, pen in hand. He began to read. When he finished, I convinced him to give me the manuscript so that I could include it in this book. My unschooled cousin has a natural talent as a writer. The following manuscript is in his own words.

Frima and Yisroel's Escape from Russia

By Irving Bogdonoff

Dated July, 2001

This message is nothing compared to the experiences of people throughout the world in their quest for freedom. It tells the experiences of a seven year old boy.

I was born in Sobolifka, a small town near Odessa. I had a younger brother who died from diphtheria. While my brother was sick, my mother tried to protect me by sending me to my father's family.

My father left for America before we got to know each other. But he corresponded with my mother. My father had four brothers. My father's father was a *stolyar*, a carpenter and a cabinet maker. He specialized in custom cabinets, window frames, and other types of furniture.

(Author's note: Both of Israel's grandfathers were carpenters. They probably knew each other, lived in neighboring towns, and arranged the marriage of their children.)

The shop was huge and full of finished products and benches. The floor was full of wood shavings. My four uncles were always looking for me under the wood shavings.

At the end of the shop stood two huge barrels. One was filled with apples to make *gus* (cider). The other was filled with tomatoes and pickles. The contents were held down with wooden lids.

(Author's note: These large wooden barrels immigrated to America with the Jews—or the idea of them did. The immigrant delicatessen owners pickled cucumbers and tomatoes in water, garlic, and a variety of spices. Many immigrant mothers made their own sour pickles and tomatoes, just as their mothers had in Europe. Even today, though sour pickles and tomatoes are found in supermarket shelves in antiseptic glass jars, the wooden barrels described by my cousin are found in the few genuine Jewish delicatessens still doing business.)

Soon after my brother died, I went back to live with my mother and her family. My grandmother was blind. She always cuddled me. My grandfather carried me close to his chest wherever he went. I had red hair, big brown eyes and lots of freckles. I hated the red hair, because it made me very conspicuous.

After my brother's death, my mother became very possessive of me and would not let me romp around with the other boys for fear I would get hurt. Mema Malka lived a few houses from my grandparents' house. Mema Malka had five children, Labela, Suma[9], Chaika, Fayga and Frayda. My cousins and I played together.

One day, Suma and I decided we did not like dogs with long tails and we decided to do something about a certain dog with a long tail. We found a brick. Suma found a rusty shovel. I held the dog with its tail centered on the brick. Suma took a swing at the tail. The dog yelped and threw me over and took off like a bolt of lightning. I never found out if we had shortened the tail.

Mema Malka's husband was a tailor. He came home on weekends, and he came on a large white horse. He worked for nobility. It was they who supplied the horse. When he left for home, he had a sack of goodies tied to the saddle.

Our house had plastered white walls, a straw roof and a dirt floor. There were no lights or plumbing. In the winter, it was bitter cold and the snow drifted over the door. It was so cold that frost formed on the inside window. The frost designs were beautiful.

My mother was also beautiful. She was tall, had a well rounded face, large brown eyes, and long black hair that she wore in a braid. Before Pesach, she would *kasher* the dishes by scalding them with hot water in a pit. In the late summer she used a cauldron to make *puvitla* for preserving. When the cider was cooking, steam ejected the *puvitla* into the air and if it landed on your face or your arms you knew what pain was.

In the winter, Labela and Suma and I went sledding. We used barrel staves for a sled. Two of us sat on a barrel

---

9   Suma is the way Israel refers to Somela (Charles).

stave and we slid down a deep path onto the icy river below.

The farmers used huge saws to cut the ice slabs and haul them away with horse teams and store them in their barns. When Christmas came, they cut out crosses and other religious symbols and placed them in the river

When spring arrived, my grandfather started taking me to *shul*. The *shul* was just big enough to accommodate the people in the town. All the women were upstairs and were separated by a thick wall with a large hole near the ceiling so the women could hear the services being conducted. In certain passages, when the women started to cry and wail, the *rebbe* would bang on the podium to quiet them. When I was about seven, I started *cheder*, but that didn't last long.

(Author's note: "did not last long," because of war, revolution and pogroms)

My mother baked bread once a week. She put extra bread on a shelf over the door. The bread was covered with a towel and it was just as fresh the last day as the first.

When food became scarce, my mother went to the *sopif* (mill) and carried a large bag of flour through the yard into the house. The flour was called *kline* or *klein*. In normal times, it was fed to animals, but we were glad to get even that. When I sat in the doorway, eating bread with honey or bread with *puvitla*, the bees bit the heck out of me.

Mother and I often walked through the open fields barefoot. Often, the cow dung was covered by the dusty wind. It is hard to imagine the feeling when you stepped on it.

The farm behind us had a huge wooden gate and animals in stalls on both sides of the enclosure. There were also fruit trees. I was always tempted by the precious cherries, plums, and apples that were begging to be picked. One day, I decided to venture forth and do some picking. I was halfway through the yard when a steer started to chase me. I ran like a deer, and managed to reach the top of the gate just as the steer crashed into it just below my feet.

One sunny day Mother was washing clothes. She ran out of water. She took me with her to the well. While drawing water, she remembered that she had left something cooking. She asked the farmer's daughter to watch me for a few minutes. The girl continued to draw the water. When the bucket was halfway up, her mother called her. The girl told me to hold the handle, and she went to her mother. I tried to bring the water laden bucket up. The tips of my fingers could not complete the arch. The steel handle slipped from my fingers. The heavy bucket started its downward track. The steel handle was whirling like a gyroplane's propeller as I tried to arrest its plunge. With my hands extended, I tried to stop the plunge, only to be hit on my forehead repeatedly.

Mother heard my screams and came running to my call. Suma, who was near my mother, followed her. When she picked me up and carried me to the house, Suma, with his hand curled, tried to catch the blood spouting into the air. In the meantime, word spread that Yisroel had fallen into the *carnitz*, the well. Everybody arrived with hooks, ropes and ladders, to rescue me. Of course, I had not fallen into the well.

The wound on my forehead did not heal properly. There was an outgrowth of flesh in the area. My mother took me to a prince who was a doctor. The doctor wanted to burn off the excess flesh with lighted cigarettes. I think they heard my screams in Odessa. I ran out of the room and my mother followed me.

One day, I got very sick. Mother tried everything to get me well, to no avail. Finally, in desperation, she decided to sell me, as was the custom. She took me to a house where they were having *minyan* services and sold me to the elders for a penny. After that, I did get better.

(Author's note: "To sell me": folk tradition. You sold a sick child so the angel of death would not find him. Another folk tradition was to go to *shul* to rename the sick person, to fool the angel of death, who was looking for someone with a different name.)

In the summer when it rained, the roads became a sea of mud. If you tried to walk, you sank to your ankles in mud. Sometimes, you walked out of your boots. The wagon wheels were buried in mud, and the farmers tied the horses' tails so that they didn't cake with mud.

In summertime in the *shtetl*, the air was fresh and smelled sweet. You felt like you were just born.

As a child, the thing that frightened me most was the wind rustling through the forest. The noise would start in the distance and pass over us with a tremendous roar.

Sobolifka had only one cobbled street and it was called the *guss*. Every Friday and Saturday night, the people gathered in the *guss*. They would *spacheer*, walk up and down, cracking garlic and pumpkin seeds under a moonlit sky. If there was a wedding, the people would gather in the evening in a corner of the marketplace. At the sound of the *chussan* breaking the glass, joy would reign and *klezmorim* would play and people danced far into the night under a moonlit sky.

In the winter, as I lay in bed, I heard the wolves howl as they gathered for the hunt. I was frightened. My mother told me to turn over a shoe and the howling would stop. In the winter time, the snow never melted. Snow simply fell on top of snow. The moon shining on the snow made the night bright as day. The cold was so intense that it was not uncommon to find the body of an unwary traveler or a drunk frozen.

The *goyim* around Halloween used to dress up in costumes and run through the community doing mischief and cutting off the hair of any woman they caught.

My father in his correspondence sent my mother money to come to America.

By this time, trouble started between the Bolsheviks and the Petliura. It turned out to be a seesaw in our town. Captive soldiers from either side would be hung from telegraph poles in the marketplace. The marketplace was a gathering place for farmers and merchants to buy, sell, or barter all kinds of merchandise. This was called a *yarid*. It occurred once a week. It was during the *yarid* that the captured soldiers were nailed to the telegraph poles while trading went on as usual.

The force that captured the town would not let the farmers leave the *yarid*. Thus, they were stranded. All the farmers wore a white *peltz*. A *peltz* was a sheepskin lined coat.

Mema Malka sold the *goyim* whiskey, which of course was illegal, but she had to make a living after her husband died.

Things did not improve. Jewish people on the road or in the street were horse whipped by the Cossacks on horseback and forced to run for their lives. The common expression that they used was "*dadit parthata*," meaning "God damn lousy Jew."

One day, Fayga, Suma, Labela and I were in the middle of the street. A couple of drunken soldiers rounded a corner and saw us there. They told us to stay there and not move. We immediately took off to a nearby cornfield and lay flat among the cornstalks while the bullets whistled overhead.

On another occasion, the soldiers were celebrating a victory and getting drunk as usual. Chaika, Mother and I were hiding in our house. After a matter of hours, Mother decided to take a peek out of the door. Just then, a mounted soldier spotted the open door and told Mother to keep it open. Dismounting, he told Mother and me to hold the horse while he went inside the house. Mother, fearing for Chaika's safety, struck the horse, causing it to run away. Then she ran into the house screaming to the soldier that his mount had run away.

(Author's note: Ida (Chaika) tells the same story: see Chapter Four.)

The soldier took off after his horse and we ran and hid in a neighbor's cellar. Sometimes we hid in cellars for days without food or water.

About this time, with civil war all around us in the *shtetl*, Mother decided to make her move and try for America. She had the money Father had sent her so she hired a *balagula* (a wagon driver) and in the company of another couple, we set out with our few possessions in a buck cart.

We traveled for weeks exposed to the elements. Even the horses were tired. When it rained, the roads were a sea of mud. We had to get out of the wagon and help push it. On hills, this was even harder. Even in dry weather, we often walked behind the wagon to ease the load and give the horses a breathing spell.

Finally, we came to a mountainous part of the country. The road headed upwards and was strewn with rocks and boulders. The road on the downgrade was even more dangerous. The front of the wagon was on the haunches of the horses. The horses were the brakes of the wagon.

I was scared, and joined the others walking behind the wagon. On one side was a solid wall of stone, on the other a drop of hundreds of feet. At the bottom we learned that the name of the town was Raskhova. It was a border town that separated the Ukraine from Romania. Mother had an aunt, Mema Brana, who lived there with her two children, a boy about 17 and a girl of 15. I don't remember their names. Raskhova was a small community surrounded by mountains. I first learned about *mamaluga* there. *Mamaluga* was a yellow cornmeal. When cooked with cheese it was very filling. Raskhova was very beautiful. The fresh mountain air filled you with energy. Everywhere you looked water sprouted out of the mountain rock. The streams were all shallow and sparkling, gathering along beaches composed of fine white granulated stone. The water in its purity had a bluish color, just like a high quality diamond. In the summer time, no matter how hot it was, the water was ice cold.

There was a horse stable about a half mile from the house. A few of the other boys in town and I always played there. In time, the man in charge got to know us. One day he asked us if we'd like to ride the horses down to the stream for a drink. We got on the horses. The downward road was narrow, flanked by a stone wall. The outer edge was a drop of about 75 feet. The horses were in single file. I was astride, nonchalant, when suddenly I realized that my horse was headed for the outer edge of the road. Frantically, I grabbed the right rein and pulled his head to the right just as he was about to step off the outer edge. Later I found out that the horse was blind in the left eye.

Raskhova was separated from Romania by a very wide and swift running river, the Dnester. It was the boundary line between the Ukraine and Romania. Both sides of the river were guarded by soldiers to preventt people from crossing it.

In order to continue this journey, we had to cross the Dnester.

My mother consulted the *rebbe* and soothsayer before our attempt to cross the river. We joined other groups that were to be guided across. We made many attempts to cross over and were repeatedly thwarted. On one occasion, the guide took the group to his cabin in the woods because it was not a good time to cross the river. The guide's cabin was near a road. Soldiers in wagons were on the lookout for people like us. Somehow, the mother of the guide got word that one of her sons, also a guide, was captured. The woman started to scream at the top of her voice. The group in the cabin was frightened, afraid that the soldiers riding on the road would hear her screams and come to arrest us. Under a moonlit sky, we all ran into the dark forest and hid. But the soldiers did not hear her screams. We all returned safely to our houses.

On another occasion while attempting to cross over, we were caught and arrested and marched to a vacant house to be held for prison or sent to Siberia. It so happened that there were quite a few attractive young girls in our group. The soldiers became obsessed with them. Mother and I, noticing the situation, slipped out the door and took off like a couple of gazelles.

In Raskhova, there being plenty of rocks, all the fences separating the houses were made up of loose rocks about four feet high. To escape the soldiers, we climbed over these loose rock fences. All the rocks tumbled after us, cutting our feet and ankles. We managed to get to Mema Brana's house. She put my mother to bed. The next day the soldiers went from house to house looking for escaped prisoners. They did not find us.

It wasn't long before we heard of a group being formed to cross the Dnester. Mother got in touch with the leader and paid our share. On the given time, we met with the group and set forth once more. It was in the dead of winter, bitter cold, and our feet crackled in the snow as we trudged along. The moon was high and beautiful. It was bright as day.

When we got to the Dnester, the river was black and forbidding from shore to shore. Anything moving on the Dnester could be seen for miles because of the white background the moon made. As we walked on the river bank, not too close together, a woman carrying a baby in her arms suddenly fell on the ice into the cold water under the thin layer of ice. Her husband grabbed the baby as his wife disappeared into the water. He slid the child across the ice, screaming for help. But the help didn't come.

We heard his screams as we struggled to cross the icy river. I tried to move away from my mother to help the man pull his wife from the slushy water. My mother grabbed me by the arm and kept me next to her. I don't know if the man saved his wife, or if he got help from others.

Now we knew that the ice was not solid. The swift water would not let the ice along the edges become solid.

People started to run in all directions to get away from the slush. I saw that those who went forward were being helped ashore by the guides. My mother grabbed my hand to pull me back the way we had come. I stopped her and insisted that we go forward. When we came to the edge of the river, the guides were helping people and carrying some ashore through the slush. But the guides were too busy with others to help us. I urged my mother to jump into the slush with me. She was frightened. But she finally gave in. We jumped in holding hands. The slush came to my chest. The current tugged at us but we managed to wade ashore. The bank was steep and composed of clay. As we scrambled up, our clothes started to freeze. The soles and heels of our shoes formed lumps. We had to stop and knock the frozen lumps off. The moon, shining in the dark forest, made every tree limb look like a soldier with a gun.

We followed our guides the better part of the night. Finally, they guided us into a sort of silo. We fell down and went right to sleep. At the crack of dawn, they woke us and led us out to a ravine and told us to continue straight ahead. They disappeared. We walked in the direction they had pointed to. Soon, we saw a few houses. My mother gently knocked on a window and a partially dressed man came outside and took us into the house. My mother was exhausted and he put her to bed. The next day the man went out to scout around. He informed us that soldiers were searching the houses and we could not stay there. He fed us and showed us the path we should follow.

His intentions were good, but we were captured. The soldiers took us to a big barn. The floor was covered with straw for us to sleep on. Two soldiers were left to guard us, and we were not allowed outside.

During our detention, we were visited by rabbis and members of various Jewish organizations. They brought us candy and news, cheer, and took any mail that we wished to forward. Sometimes they even brought us clothes. We were imprisoned in that straw-filled barn for seven months. Then, we started to hear rumors that we would be released. The rumors turned out to be true. We were released through efforts of Jewish organizations.

My mother got a job as a domestic in a wealthy house. I hid in the garden while she worked.

Mother wrote to my father. He sent us money, and paid the ship passage for us to come to America. It was not long after that that we headed for Hamburg, the port of embarkation.

As a child, I picked up the language in any country we passed through. I suppose it was due to the length of time that we spent in each country.

On the set day for embarking, in September, 1922, I was sick. Our ship was the Finland. We had to pass through Customs. I had a high fever. Mother was afraid that we would not be allowed on the ship because I was sick. I insisted that we go, for if we missed the boat we would have to wait six months for another boat. Mother followed my advice. When I stood in front of the doctor who examined everyone before they boarded the boat, he looked at my flushed face and large eyes, patted me on the head and said that boys played too hard. No sooner did we get on board when mother threw me into bed. I stayed in bed for a week. When I finally got on deck, it was so foggy you could not see the person a few feet in front of you. The ship's horn was blasting constantly and I felt like a pea in a thick soup.

We traveled second class. The American tourists were separated from us by two small strings in the dining room. Everything else was the same as first class.

After two weeks, we arrived in New York. My father was there to greet us and we boarded the train to Philadelphia, where my father had settled.

My father took us to our new home, which was a small store and a "dwelling" where we lived. Our first address was 2100 South Beechwood Street.

The store opened at 6 A.M. The first thing Pop did was to dry the salt and icy water from the ice cream cabinet and get it ready for the truck to come with the new shipment of ice cream and salt. We used 15 to 20 buckets of ice cream daily, depending on the weather.

We were in the gas era, gas jets and gas mantles.

The store was located in an American Irish neighborhood. The bums used to show my father a hard time. Around Easter, they threw eggs into our windows and store.

I had to fight my way home from school and every time I stuck my head outside the house.

My brothers, Morris and Philip, were both born in that house.

My father rented the building and after 16 years was given notice to move. Pop bought a corner grocery store in an all colored (Black) neighborhood.

My parents could not read or write English. They could only sign their names. The task of ordering from Penn Mutual fell to me.

(Author's note: Penn Mutual was a Philadelphia collective that preceded supermarkets and provided small store owners lower wholesale prices.)

I often went to Dock Street with my father to buy fruits and vegetables.

(Author's note: Dock Street, on the shores of the Delaware River, was the wholesale area where small business owners purchased fresh food every day, usually before dawn.)

We had plenty of competition. There were stores like ours on every corner. We worked very hard.

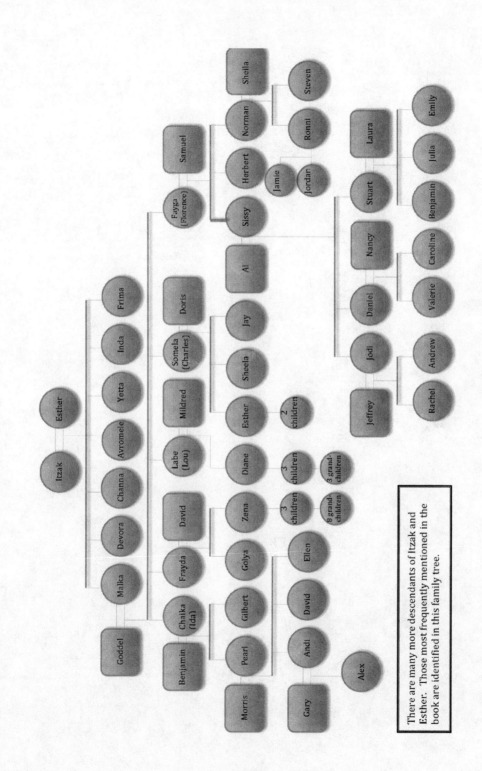

There are many more descendants of Itzak and Esther. Those most frequently mentioned in the book are identified in this family tree.

223

CPSIA information can be obtained at www.ICGtesting.com
Printed in the USA
LVOW05s2059100813

347265LV00003B/350/P

9 781440 177224